The Returns: Collected Poems

Also by Alfred Corn

POETRY
Unions
Tables
Contradictions
Stake: Selected Poems, 1972-1992
Present
Autobiographies
The West Door
Notes from a Child of Paradise
The Various Light
A Call in the Midst of the Crowd
All Roads at Once

NOVELS
Miranda's Book
Part of His Story

CRITICISM
Arks & Covenants
Atlas: Selected Essays, 1989-2007
The Poem's Heartbeat: A Manual of Prosody
The Metamorphoses of Metaphor

The Returns

COLLECTED POEMS

ALFRED CORN

Press 53
Winston-Salem

Press 53, LLC
PO Box 30314
Winston-Salem, NC 27130

First Edition

Silver Concho Poetry Series
edited by Pamela Uschuk & William Pitt Root

Cover design by Kevin Morgan Watson

Poems from *Contradictions* reprinted
by permission from Copper Canyon Press

Poems from *Unions* reprinted
by permission from Barrow Street Books

Library of Congress Control Number
2022932469

Printed on acid-free paper
ISBN 978-1-950413-41-6

For Marilyn Hacker and Mimi Khalvati,
guild masters and companions along the road

Acknowledgments

Earlier volumes include a complete list of magazine appearances, but I would like to thank some of those magazines (and their editors) that consistently found room for my work over the decades. In particular: *The New Yorker*, *The New York Review of Books*, *The Nation*, *The New Republic*, *Poetry Review* (U.K.), *The Georgia Review*, *Poetry*, *The Hudson Review*, *The Wolf* (U.K.), *The Paris Review*, *Slate*, *The Yale Review*, *Sagarana* (Italy), *The Boston Review*, *PN Review* (U.K.), *Salmagundi*, *Poetry London*, *Cutthroat*, *The New England Review*, *Letras Libres* (Mexico).

I am also grateful to writer friends who were willing to offer comments on early drafts of the poems. They include Richard Howard, Grace Schulman, Edmund White, Marilyn Hacker, Robert Pinsky, and Joel Connaroe.

It very much pleases me that Pam Uschuk and William Pitt Root believed that this volume belonged in the Silver Concho Poetry Series they edit. For his excellent work as the publisher of Press 53, I thank Kevin Morgan Watson. Also, I am grateful to my agent Tom Miller, whose warm support and hard work has helped smooth the path to publication.

Contents

Preface

Nearly a quarter-century ago, I brought out the volume *Stake: Selected Poems, 1972-1992*. Even then there was one book I hadn't included poems from, and since that time, three more have appeared. It seems appropriate now to bring out a second selection, pruning the earlier one and adding to it. Because of space constraints, I have (just as in *Stake*) omitted the prose documents that were interleaved with lyrics in the poem sequence "A Call in the Midst of the Crowd." Because they are fully effective only when read complete, I have not included excerpts from the book-length poem *Notes from a Child of Paradise*, nor from the long sequence "1992" found in *Autobiographies*. My hope is that readers, stimulated by the present selection, will look elsewhere for these omitted works. The earlier selection appeared with a longish introduction that I think is mostly still applicable. Except for minor errors and misprints, the poems collected here are identical to those in earlier books. I am grateful that this selection will make a part of my work available to a new generation of readers.

Alfred Corn
Providence, Rhode Island
December 24, 2021

ALL ROADS AT ONCE
(1976)

Promised Land Valley, June '73

The lake at nightfall is less a lake,
but more, with reflection added, so
this giant inkblot lies on its side,
a bristling zone of black pine and fir
at the dark fold of the revealed world.

Interpret this fallen symmetry,
scan this water and these water lights,
and follow a golden scribble toward
the lantern, the guessed boat, the voices
that skip across sky to where we stand.

You are vanishing and so am I
as everything surrenders color,
falling silent to vision. Darkness
rises to drown out the sky and silence
names us to the asking boat.

Who echoes who in the black mirror?
Riddles are answers here at the edge.
And still, we can imagine some clear call,
a spoken brilliance blazing the trail . . .
ourselves moving out across the sky.

An Oregon Journal

I

Afternoon: the waves are pure change when the tide
turns, and the defeated eye pulls back
to drop anchor in rock. Deserted by water,
the cliff base was a drying seascape of
green anemones and steel-blue mussel shoals
crackling in the painful flood of air.
Then the predators, marigold and liver-pink
stars fallen in dancers' poses in rock pools,
flattened against barnacle crusts.
                                        You are
there now, made large by time, observing;
the expansive hair stirs, relaxes.
You picked up an empty mussel shell, still twinned,
and offered me half, old tarnished spoon,
the thumb-sized hollow pearled in gray rainbows.
Something in your looks or the thinning light
says we won't always be together.
Back there, top-heavy clusters of white
everlastings tap against the sea breeze.
I don't think you saw them, or me, testing
the bone-hard blade of the shell. I tried
to break it, then threw it back to the great
factory of ocean where it will be
ground up and recast as kelp, fish, bird,
star—or another instance of itself.

II

                                    The temperatures
appeared, then a snow-blue delirium,
possibly the source of the first images:
to step out at night on to audible sands,
mind brooming aside hazes above

the tossing surfaces, to feel fever against
the silhouettes of rocks.
                                        A milk moon,
no, a broken aspirin changing leaden mist
into platinum with its sour light.
                                                    We saw
the reflection of a salty star in the wet,
this side the reach of the waves . . . .
Not recollected in tranquility;
as if we could ever rest and the waves
not echo in our inner ear, high tides
not come forward in feeling change. The best
themes are the moving ones, those closest
following the skating hand that records,
balance, the motive of figure and line.
      My eyes dilated, I tugged the threads
of daydream texts as each day passed
and our night clock, moon-dial, grew fat
with the time we spent.

III

Morning and a garden path: leaves looking
edible as lettuce except for their saw-
toothed margins that promised bitter green juice.
Hydrangeas, huge indigo sponges,
the fleshy petals sopping with dew.
Flushes of lavender—one deliquescent
bloom, bending drunkenly on its stem,
bopped my shoulder as I passed, a morning
shower. . . .
                  I said, during our walk
to the woods above the sea, "Only two things
make life worth the trouble—
One is love."
                    "The other?"
                                        "Memory."
It seemed true—how else get past the dead
stretches of time without opening the album

of faded pictures, old fumbles, old dances?
Without the touch and spark of skin, sheets, the dim
fireplaces of half-closed eyes? Always less feverish
than I, you suggested, "Conversation. Art.
Food. Drink." A reasonable summary.
    We climbed an unfamiliar hill, lit
with leaf-filtered silver; practiced naturism,
love, memory. Staring as we moved into
the sun—a huge brass flower opening in my head,
daylight shocked into stillness.
                                                    I lay back
to take in the changes, resting in
my thoughts, who couldn't know yours. Above,
flimsy poles, topped with tepees of evergreen—
the firs swayed, lightsome, stirred again
quietly in the easy breeze. It was blue
beyond, but the clearest indigo, an essential
ink. So we lay. A hummingbird took
our clothes for flowers in the even green
and brown about us. It flew up with copter
motions; hesitated, perplexed at the cloth,
and left as it came.

IV

At noon: a Japanese salad of brown kelp
crunched underfoot. Up toward the dry,
driftwood, abandoned sculptures, antique
metals deeply scratched according to the grain.
The sand changes right before our eyes,
wide-wale corduroy, dry drapery, cross-
patterns in dull gray moire. Everything is
moment, the colors, the lines. We invent
the world and a wide cup to catch it in:
I saw tough, beautiful sea grass rooted
in thinnest sand, and wanted to say it.
Moving discoveries, fever, sand-flow,
voices demanding form for days
that have forgotten their colors. . . .

It began there, among the changing blues
and scored silver. I will make something,
bright lines for mine or someone's use,
light from other worlds breaking on this one.

V

The drive to the interior—other trees.
Landscapes, green surfaces punched through by
country rooftops shingled in satin-gray.
Maples were putting out the first yellow,
and we pass a non-town the signs call
Remote.
            So tiring always to drive downhill!
Myrtles and spruces filed past, unhurried.
I recognized the red-skinned madrone,
a sort of myth-tree, one a child
might have drawn. It seemed out of place
there among the elegant constructions
of spruce and fir. The conifers, so old
they are out of time, stand ever new, blue,
sempiternal Xmas trees.

VI

An inland cemetery:
at the summit of a long, hot hill,
reddish earth and brown oak leaves; a grave
formality of tilting stones dated
in sixties and eighties. "Mr. Daniel—
His Death Made Heaven More Necessary."
We disputed the interpretation of it.
      Not far, under the ragged shade
of a moss-eaten madrone, a rotting stone
choked under a tangle of vetch. Some
bleached plastic flowers starved in the sandy ground,
chartreuse and pink. I guessed the true complexion
of death, almost laughed, and then I heard

the rattle of locusts in the heated weeds. Were they
poisonous snakes? I was glad to feel fear
again—no thanks to death, who makes living
almost unnecessary.
                                    We each looked
for monuments with our names. You found one.
Thoughts were locusts as I sat and watched them,
pinpoints darting among the indifferent trees.
When we left, the stones were sorry we couldn't stay.

VII

Stopping in a hotel, arbitrary room
of closure. Everything finds margin
in shaded zones—sea, love, time past.
The journal could serve as anchor,
fixity of fact in the great blur. It was
this way, except for omissions, concessions
to tact, daydream, form; and the singling out
of persistent detail, changes, electric
blues and silvers—the way you later find
a thread in a texture that seemed nothing
but puzzles and tangles.
                                    Will I ever stay
in that room again? The proofs of the past
are still washing in, manuscript crowded
with change, curly with deletions. Someone
pauses, resting a hand on the silver
knob, trying to remember precisely.
But instinct, deferring to a final
revision, waits and leaves the door ajar.
The ocean says the past is a project
To be continued.

Chinese Porcelains at the Metropolitan

It was as though I had stumbled
On an unrecognized need, this
Rich embarrassment . . . . For once, I really looked,
Pressing the glass that defended them,
My native state, my own feelings—from what
Source—caught up in and congruent

To the bulge and flow of those forms,
Splendid in unimaginable
Glazes: *clair-de-lune*, *mirror-black*, *tea-dust*,
Celadon, *ox-blood*, *famille noire*, *peach-bloom*,
Imperial yellow, *café-au-lait*,
Fish-roe crackle, and *blue-and-white*.

This last one was its own country—
Silken pillars of milk dribbled
With a blue syrup that slid down those hard
White slopes, improbably assuming real
Shapes: a branch, ravaged with plum blossoms,
A house, man, or frightened dragon.

Then, *famille noire*: I was confused
At finding myself a moment
In someone else's dream, as a drooping
Peony explodes; spring through sunglasses,
Onyx skies, the threat of a striped wing. That
Was plenty. I retreated to

An unfigured vase of clear green:
Near-real pear or ideal teardrop,
It seemed to lean up against weight, solid
Impetus, recording the smooth action
Of the potter's wheel that hidden still whirred
In the risen gyre of the form.

Form and color, ancient, modern
Captors, saying a shape in clay
Can trace the curve of largest concerns, brim
And not overflow with a full version
Of self . . . . I read the supple script of those
Lines, poems across the trenches

Of time: *You've met the past and it is*
Present. The struggle has not ended,
Will not end. Meaning is only a moment
Contained; but form is legion. The rainbow lists
Go on as new invasions spin up from dream.
Everything still remains to be done.

Parable at a Roman Fountain

How can the statues not touch each other,
Hands, breasts, thighs, slickened by water,
Flesh perfected from the flesh that dies as grass?
Change here is only eternal, like white
Noise, stone trance guarded in a cage of glass
Parabolas, barring the Roman night;
It seems light in a watery medium
Has baptized them free of motion and time.

We stand at the rim in rapt attitudes,
Admiring the secular prisoners
From the vantage point assigned to lovers;
And think we detect old glimmers of grief
And envy in a marble eye—the cold nudes
Tempted, for love, to dress themselves in life.

The Bridge, Palm Sunday, 1973

It avails not, time nor place—distance avails not...

—Whitman, "Crossing Brooklyn Ferry"

The bridge was a huge sentence diagram,
You and I the compound subject, moving
Toward the verb. We stopped, breathing
Balloonfuls of air, and the sun made itself felt
As a hard spray of light. Sensing an occasion,
II put my arm on your shoulder, my friend
And brother. Words today took the form of actions.

The object of the pilgrimage, 110 Columbia Heights,
Where Hart Crane used to live, no longer existed—
No such number, no physical address. The only
Available tribute was to read his poem
There on the Promenade in sight of the theme.
The line moved you about the bedlamite whose shirt
Balloons as he drops into the river; much like
Crane's death, though he wasn't a "bedlamite";
A dreamer, maybe, who called on Whitman and clasped
His present hand, as if to build a bridge across time. . . .

We hadn't imagined happenstance would lead us next
To join with the daydreamers lined up before
An Easter diorama of duck eggs, hatching
Behind plate glass. The intended sentiment featured
Feathered skeletons racked with spasms of pecking
Against resistant shell, struggling out of dim
Solitary into incandescence and gravity, and quaking
With the shock of sound and sight as though existence
Were a nervous disease. All newborns receive the same
Sentence—birth, death, equivalent triumphs.

Two deaf-mutes walked back the same but inverse way,
Fatigue making strangers of us and the afternoon
Hurt, like sunburn. Overexposure is a constant
Risk of sensation and of company. I wondered
Why we were together—is friendship imaginary?
And does imagination obscure or reveal its subject?
The ties always feel strange, strung along happenstance,
Following no diagram, incomplete, a bridge of suspense.

Sometimes completed things revisited still resonate.
I'm thinking about Crane's poem of the Bridge,
Grand enough to inspire disbelief and to suspend it.
The truth may lie in imagining a connection
With him or with you; with anyone able to overlook
Distance, shrug off time, on the right occasion . . . .

If I called him a brother—help me with this, Hart—
Who climbed toward light and sensation until the sky
Broke open to reveal an acute, perfect convergence
Before letting him fall back into error and mortality—
Would we be joined with him and the voyagers before
him?
Would a new sentence be pronounced, a living connection
Between island and island, for a second, be made?

Pages from a Voyage

I

Friends tell me in partly concealed shock
To "build myself up"—by which I gauge
Distances come, the skull pushing out
On its voyage through flesh. All the work
Of elusive viruses during the dark
Two months of this year. Stowaways,
Saboteurs, the worst of them have jumped ship,
Leaving me to convalesce, kill time
With reading (from Darwin's *Voyage*), thinking.
Strange, considering that thought itself may be
A disease when one decides perversely
And with a familiar sinking sensation
To get to the bottom of everything. . . .
Don't ask me what my motive was.

What would Darwin have answered?
Adventure? Knowledge? A journal entry
From Cape Verde, his first port: "The scene,
As beheld through the hazy atmosphere
Of this climate, is of great interest;
If, indeed, a person, fresh from the sea,
And who has just walked, for the first time,
In a grove of cocoa-nut trees, can be a judge
Of anything but his own happiness."
An auspicious beginning; also shore leave
Was a holiday from his perpetual
Seasickness; from bad food, close quarters.
Maybe he should have asked that fair island
Moment to stay: he will return to England
An invalid, imaginary, or perhaps really suffering
Undiagnosed from Chagas's disease.

What am I suffering from?
A fevered imagination, to begin with.
Waiting for health is a painful game
Of patience or like painting by numbers:
Art as patient therapy, but not always
With therapeutic results. I drink tea
With honey; look around my place and see
Repairs are needed; but don't do them.
When the holidays from fever come,
I go out, do errands, charm back normality;
That is, try to recognize it.

But the city, the air, the crowds,
Tone-rows of car horns caught in traffic—
Cacophony? Music? This is the world
We inherited from him. I'm adrift,
Guilty of dereliction. A mendicant,
I scan each face as it passes,
If this one might offer some response,
Feeling, intelligence. (A mistake
To try such an experiment in this city,
I know that.) Mostly one sees
Vanity, interest, in the bad sense;
Sometimes lust in action, unwelcome now.
Or vacuity: faces, eyes, shallow saucers
Any lukewarm broth can be poured into
And held for a while. It seems
Everyone asks to be deceived.

Some of the women at least seem comfortable—
These hardy young mothers in pants and canvas
Shoes, guiding the unruly strollers just ahead;
Comparing notes on childhood and the big
Questions: Sex, Age, Health, the Phases.
Almost unconscious, they've lost interest
In appearance; wear no make-up; cut
Their own hair, shorter than men's.

Who are these goddesses and what is
The immense power behind the carriages?
Hard to believe any human she, fully
Comprehending the grade and length of pushing
One of those babies all the way to adulthood,
Wouldn't run screaming into the night. . . .
But they get through, one day at a time.
Childless, I can only guess at that day.

Finally one is reduced to life,
The conditions of life: what matters?
Where am I deceived?
Irresistible gravity of truth
Drawing us forward, deeper into the future,
Whatever the conclusions.
The Darwin who returns after five years
Holds title to the name of a stranger
Who began the voyage. . . .

The Ages of Man are always beginning,
Everything reshuffled, yes, and just when
Youthful optimism, gone senile, retires
From active duty. Each age a maiden
Voyage; and who still feels eligible?
I live days of strange complexion;
Thought stumbles on many moods and words
Come in curious ways, the language
Of discovery and emergency.

For diversion, I see paintings:

II
Mortefontaine
J.-B.-C. Corot

Feather-grey, and bending left of true,
A tree rises from the heart of matter,
Shade for water, recreation, dreams.
The place is speckled with lacquered leaves,
Light-flecks scattered casual as grain.

Sun infuses the general cloud,
The lake a pearled cloud also enjoined
To symmetry in which the temple
Twins, improbable here—as the boatman
Mooring a shallop behind the birch

Is not. Unaware of him she does
Needlework. Outdoors? But the painting belongs
To fiction, not truth . . . . It's puzzling, the charm
Of an ideal that does not reflect
The bare, actual life at hand.

He perfected the world; but I resist
And will not see symmetry if none is
There. The charm's broken, diversion spoiled.
His mirror shows my own reverses. Life
Is breath: the world clouds over, gray with loss.

III
A Separation

The errand that brought me here is clear enough,
But what made me turn just now, eyes filling
With the sunset over the blue park, the hidden river?
Trees of no leaf; half light assumed to be sun,
A pale yellow with silhouettes of branches.

Come back unspoken bends upward with suppliant limbs—
Addressed to memory. This was our turf. One of these streets
Led us down to the park as often as weather allowed;
Even when it didn't. For example, there was that rainy spring
Toward the end, your mother off on the *Beagle* tour
Of the Galapagos, the forecast here so discouraging;
My hand nonetheless dabbled in the stream of a passing
Hedge . . . . We stopped to acknowledge rainwashed irises
That fleurdelised a bed along the way.

One of these comes back as emblem for all—
A hum, a blue daze, no actual color;
And a suspicion of lemon creeping out
From the throat, spreading over a tongue
Printed with ramified blue.
We always admired the same things. . . .
No, not always. Memory grimaces, goes sour.
In fact, we often disagreed. You weren't prepared
For a symbolist's habits of mind, I imagine.

Beauty's inadequacy to the world: a proposition
Dismissed or countered by careful selection,
Crossing the fine and fragile with the plain and hardy. . . .
Even at this moment the vestigial aesthetic eye fastens
On what might be a huge petal, veined with branches
And hanging from the iris of midwinter sky; I could see it
As an emblem, the blue and gold complex of what we were.
But the emblem doesn't quite do the job, I know that.

Enough. What would have been seen at one time fails to satisfy me now. Once I might have used lateness and my errand to suggest the flight of time and the doomed quest for an always more distant past. Experience arranged in a splendid contraption. . . . But no. It's literally late and I do have an errand, not related to the past. To tell the truth, I can only guess who we were; it's been too long. What's most present now is the suspicion that beautiful emblems are a kind of lotus-eating, myths that mask the truth. (I feel agreement rush in from all sides.) And yet, avoiding the gorgeous, adopting the plain and hardy, do we finally get the truth? I wonder if that might not just give us one more mask, another myth . . . . It's not in this frame of mind poems are written, and, indeed, there's no poem here. These are only midwinter thoughts, another effort to come to terms with us; or with terms themselves, which, I suppose, should be means and not ends.

IV
To a Friend, from a Landing

The hours spent here accumulate like building blocks
Exactly the cube of your black-walled living room.
Consideration increased in a repeated setting:
Glass and chrome, flowers, ice, white sofa, clay elephant.
Often there was music or reading. The good life, no?
I reviewed each print suspended on your invisible walls;
Difficulty wasn't part of the picture, apparently.

You're at your post in the rocker; everything should be
Normal but conversation lumbers, elephant-like, weighted
With memory. (When was it you gave me the Moorehead book
On Darwin? You thought I'd like the toucan pictures.)
Consider the ruins of the afternoon—spilled ashes,
Chaos among crumbling towers of books and albums.
Surface disorder: but surfaces are often profound.
We're both subdued, reduced; both changing, we say.
Still, there's tea, whole-wheat toast, honey—
Amenities. We nibble and sip; and I ask how
The yoghurt-maker's doing. And is Spenser
Really good? Deliberate questions, deliberate answers.
Caught in the comedy of change, it's as though each
Spoken word is meant to stay mutability, its terrors.

We struggle to compose some device of sincerity—
A device, two-dimensional, emblazoned on armor,
But distinguishing friend from foe. We struggle,
And, frankly, we'd like to go back to small talk.
But you have never been so present before:
A whole room funneled into moving gray eyes.
I put down the cup, not knowing whether to go or stay.
I'm thinking about the life of friendship, good and bad,
A mixture of pleasure, misreadings, shared jokes,
And the blind, inept desire to be shield and ally,
Equal to the changes time accumulates in us. . . .
I can't find a device to say this, not yet.
At a turning point, covered with confusion, I make
My escape; but reluctant to go. I'm on the landing;
We shout and laugh, cheerful, friendly, stranded.

V

Collecting its virulent specimens,
Could the expedition go too far?
Think of Darwin feeding the Benchuga bug
With his own blood and contracting himself
To a lifelong disease—all for knowledge.
Belief torpedoed; and history
Hasn't recovered yet. Not that a credo
Drawn from the mortal body is beyond hope;
Just that time is short, the poison spreading.

After 1859 Europe makes steadily
Toward materialism: Darwin, then Nietzsche,
'Social Darwinism,' *laissez-faire*, Fascism,
Ethnology, Man the Hunter and Killer.
Darwin's little finches quickly evolve
Into chimeras all with a common ancestry
Of good intentions. Case in point:
The eloquent enemy of slavery
Becomes a source book of racism.

Good intentions; and still the scientist
Is fascinated by murderous nature:
"One day, at Bahia, my attention was drawn
By observing many spiders, cockroaches,
And other insects, and some lizards, rushing
In the greatest agitation across a bare piece of ground.
A little way behind, every stalk and leaf
Was blackened by a small ant. The swarm
Having crossed the bare space, divided itself,
And descended an old wall. By this means
Many insects were fairly enclosed; and the efforts
Which the poor little creatures made
To extricate themselves from such a death
Were wonderful."

VI

We move toward our opposite;
Opposite except for a thin film,
A membrane of experience. Biography,
Like history, repeats itself, a pendulum,
Or like tacking zigzags into the wind,
The sawblade of a risky expedition,
Version plotted by dead reckoning:
The ship moves out to the edge of the world.

For Darwin, several sightings of death—
Encounters with Indians, rounding the Horn;
Or the earthquake at Concepción:
"A bad earthquake at once destroys
Our oldest associations: the earth,
The very emblem of solidity, has moved
Beneath our feet like a thin crust
Over a fluid;—one second of time
Has created in the mind a strange idea
Of insecurity, which hours of reflection
Would not have produced."

This season only accelerated a process
Always under way; as though fever
Fired the boiler of some
Auxiliary engine—forward
With all speed until the block cracks.
It was a premonition of shipwreck.
After days dimmed with fever,
And two nights brilliant with sleeplessness,
It began to pound, loud
As a throttle, a mechanical thing.

All night, again no sleep. By morning,
Complete, jerky exhaustion.

Stumbling on sea legs to the bathroom mirror:
A gauntness, bones cased in waxy flesh.

Dull, dead eyes, no feeling.
I felt a kind of abstract compassion:

No one should have to go through this,
No human being . . . . which came

Only because of the certainty
That it could not be me,

This dead face. Otherwise
Pride, refusing to pity

Would have interfered; an absurd
Scruple at that moment.

No one should have to—but they do, and worse.
Eventually a pill dragged me under.

VII
A Foretaste

Down to the water, in no hurry.
Stood and looked across.
Neither tempted or untempted.
A landscape reduced to signature.
Waited and watched. Considered
The last water and the useless sky.
Then turned and came back.
I remember this dream in characters.

There's a special queer radiance now—
Notice an open milk carton, or lettuce
Drying in the colander; a ray of light
Crossing the floor in afternoon.
Also, a mistrust of things:
The colors are paler, experience
Frangible, like weathering limestone.
It's all ready to collapse into chalky ruin.

VIII

The Galapagos, Melville's *Encantadas*—
Carapaces of bubbled rock and black sand,
"Glowing hot"; they supported lichen, cactus.
Here evolving suspicions hardened into certainty.
It anticipates our own reptilian landscape.

The tortoises: man-tall necks, mournful faces,
Every day a transport. They take their trailers
To the waterholes and tank up a month's quota.

Mating comes as a collision of armored cars.
Barring crack-ups and slaughter, they are immortal.

Or the lizards: cold-blooded half-smiles
Swaddled in slack leather. Harmless.
But nonplussed by these curious observers.
Darwin grabs the tail of a burrower:
"At this it was greatly astonished,
And soon shuffled up to see what was the matter;
And then stared me in the face, as much
As to say, 'What made you pull my tail?'"

Reading this paragraph, I can see its genial author.
I hesitate; I clasp the hand of a friend.
That, and the rest, force me to will his book,
And along with it, the consequences;
According to the practices of friendship
Among scattered witnesses across date and place;
Introductions arranged by books;
The true heritage, where descent
Is called tradition, culture
A sea of competing species:
Only the fittest survive,
But those for all generations.

Lines inscribed in blood,
Chromosomes of word
Coupled at the crossing
Of tradition, mutation,
Generate a book—

Form fit to the purpose,
Source reborn as a new
Origin, living afterwards,
Mating with kindred minds;
Breed true, sole offspring of mine.

IX

The future attracts with the help of ignorance.
It's hard to believe he would have made the voyage
If he had known the consequences. Still, it would
Have been a shame to miss the Andes, their fossil
Shells; the bland, unearthly bromeliads;
Ostrich dumplings; the coconut-eating crab;
The flamingos and their hieroglyphic reflections
At sunset waterholes; the tattooed Maoris. . . .

Summing up the value for future voyagers:
"In a moral point of view, the effect ought to be,
To teach him good-humoured patience, freedom
From selfishness, the habit of acting for himself,
And of making the best of every occurrence."
Maybe so. I've made the best of it I could;
And this morning I find myself saying
As my sum that the point is to realize we do
What we do—to have it 'happen,' beautiful
Or terrible. It seems that the choice between bliss
And knowledge is no choice at all,
Not for the species of Adam.

Sickness and health coexist unjustified,
Become a part of each other.
There's something electric about life—
One feels protective of its ignorant optimism.
The body, like a child, doesn't know
About meaninglessness or death;
It's ready for dinner or a kiss.

Things always begin. There is
A pile of fresh-stamped letters to mail;
The back of a neck to squeeze;
Nails to be hammered with well-judged strokes;
A shirt fallen on the floor in an expressive

Attitude; and the way a ribbon of poured honey
Folds backward and forward on itself. . . .
So many minds to become, events that might be
Beheld, the heart of matter through which a conditional
World springs colored, solid; seizes there.

I'm feeling pressure now
From the suspect messianic;
But intentions here were mostly good,
And the record at least recognizable.
I feel—alive. There's been a reprieve, this
Surprised minding of the glad sense in things. . . .
Everything is still moving, and it's possible
To consider other voyages over the rim,
Incautiously curious about the animals,
The unclassified flowers of the future.
This round goes to me.

A CALL IN THE MIDST OF THE CROWD
(1978)

The Adversary

I

In cold spring, a bird of passage, species
You don't recognize, precedes you, just as
The hills retreat into dusk or fog, blurring
Toward the last color. What I might have said—
But the heart's gone out of it, so that
Late footprints only fill with mud, blunted
Purpose. Removed in the house of your thoughts
You hear nothing. A word falls from parted lips
Revealed in the dim light as almost half
A world; though you by force of being everywhere
Never appear. Who believes he follows his own
Intentions, if all of them end with you? Again
The city raises its trophies among the clouds,
A final myth. Nothing left but the desire
To speak the truth. This is yours, the silver
Cord is severed, and the case reopens.

II

You survive, you have accommodated
The miracle, and nothing was transfigured.
Your mind, the cold day, the hills
Flatten to scenery, just as expected.
For only to appearances are you wise.
You see them as a given, disorders
Mankind is heir to, clinically named, each
An oasis, possibly mirage, marking
A listless horizon. Old harmonies, reconciled
Nature, accuse one's errors of spirit.
You hesitate over the next step, a habit
Contagious as cold, the subject forced
To keep mentally indoors, light off the snow
Discovering each outline, multiplying
Possibility until—until your mood changes.
Would you know me in some other guise,

Still mirror, you there, intending no
Special malice, who, neat and impartial,
Blight what you touch? The drama did not unfold
In a temple, your premises drab and general,
Contact a dumb show, the stratagems
Of performance and policy, coming and going.
I wanted to take life to my lips like
The simple water—and your hand intervenes.

III

Surely I've seen you before, the candid
Eyes, poised head marbled by thought as air
By smoke? And you called them, family
Of dreams that descend in slippers
The carpeted stair, fatal company, one
After one? You withhold what you know, as
Substance begins to rub away, mist from glass.
If this were repose, no complaint; but
Something stings, an inevitable drop
Of acid in the solution. The cold hills
Wait for us, spring's coming on strong.
Nothing left but the desire to speak the truth,
Drawn by the power that lies in discredit.
Where are you going? You look pale, the glare
Goes up in volume, drowning you out. I am
To understand: Nothing human is alien to you;
And so you are mortal. The black tunnel roars
And suddenly opens out into space

Winter Stars

E quindi uscimmo riveder le stelle.
—*Inferno, xxxiv*

In winter also, climbing up
From underground he sees them,
Each one a tear of light that falls
From beasts or heroes unconsidered

In cities till the traveler
Stops, looks up, and then remembers
Their names—who will infuse his eye,
Its dark pool silvered with cloud and stars.

From an Album

for Sandy

As though becoming actual light
Created what it revealed or is
A new element to be drawn in
And made one substance with us both, now
That you in a single instance catch
The world's mind, passion our witness
For what has always remained to be proved.
The first gleam shines where least expected—
Small inner revolutions, beginnings
That break loose to move upward, energies
Radiantly dispersing. . . . The familiar
Deities, all their contending wills, gather
Like planets to ask, How do I know this?
As a far cry, by pure possibility.
That world of objects perpetually
Closes in, a curtain only parted
At the rare moment when seeing comes of age.
Mornings in color, daylight and daybreeze
Return your image in a space of the first
Water, ourselves an added dye of instinct,
Reproving time gratefully ignoring it.
One last farewell, and then we have begun.

A Call in the Midst of the Crowd

Poem in Four Parts on New York City

JANUARY

Night swallows up everything but doesn't
Alone cast the shadow inside, this sense
Of incompleteness, lack
Of echo. . . . I expect
Too much? Too little? My undetailed season
Only appears in the bright particulars
Of paired headlights flooding an avenue,
You'd say, at cross-purposes with Number.
If the worst certainties were skill—but now
Down comes to out, and words crumble, refuse
To sign their names, empty noises rattling
A barrenness their failure parallels.
People, like a people, do have slumps, when
Nothing wants to be said, and what is,
Hardly worth anyone's staying awake for:
A satire for unaccommodated men.

Best, they claim, to remount the horse that threw
You (in the present case, a horse with wings),
An act demonstrating,
Proving that you are—what?
I've forgotten. Reach, grasp; moth, star; and
"He's the very wishbone he breaks in two."
How to sustain it, the doubtful subject
Of a self in neither sense exemplary?
In those doorways a man will freeze tonight,
Disappointment's victim, failure at love,
Dazed, benumbed—hardly more than expression.
Sheer perversity, I guess, makes me plumb
The mirror of this self-imposed city for
What, if anything here, holds a promise,
The speaking gift that falls to one who hears
A word shine through the white noise of the world.

Midnight Walk, St. Marks Place

Biography repeats itself. Couples break
Apart. This could be that same winter spent
Just down the street, a short walk from the grave
Of Peter Stuyvesant; our divorce pending,
Cheerless tippling, useless midnight phone calls,
The commonplaces of pain—which makes us
Anybody. Now, chance brings me here again:
The buildings in dead Auden's neighborhood
Discovering their age,
The cornices revealed
As snow eyebrows over extinct windows.
Snow underfoot; and notice how snow not
Muffles but makes a miniature of sound,
The tiny scrape of a shovel on concrete,
The barest hush as my breathing out turns
Into frost. Walking alone, one hears things.

Times like now, a life moves forward one foot
Before the other and by discipline
Alone—Auden's practice year after year,
You can tell. A willed punctuality.
Look, I've come as far as
The Astor Colonnades,
Mansions let fall into ruin, along with
Any number of encumbering passions. . . .
Now snow falls down in fistfuls, clabbering
The slopes of cars into anonymity—
A transport to simpler times, that pale gold
Window lit not electrically; and here
A blue spruce thrown out after Epiphany.
But those tinsel icicles, windblown sidewise,
Are strictly post-World War, like me. And times
Are simpler now, really. Just what's wrong with them.

Nine to Five

The first days of the new year go on trial,
Destinies sluggishly reassumed
As handed down, the summons delivered
By the thrilling of predawn alarms. . . .
Radios follow you down the stairwell,
Sound from apartments like rival perfumes—
Symphonies, pop tunes, talk shows and weather.
A day surprised by rain, which falls down viscous,
Almost snow. Your umbrella snags on awnings
Or locks horns with others', and there a broken
One lies like Dracula dead on the sidewalk,
Silk heart pierced by a silver
Ferrule. No one comments
Though chatter precedes you, enters, and fills
An elevator as doors close with steely
Conviction. Now the several perfumes

Blend, no, clash like rival radios. . . . And
Will the sentence of connecting rooms ever
Be understood, the dull fluorescent glare,
Standard desks, floors and machines, routine
Greetings and drab coffee, the undertone
Of sex and violence? Backstabbing and lust
As antidotes to boredom:
Kill time; but don't seem to.
From your window tarpaper rooftops blacken
And silver under a grainy fallout
Of gusting sleet. There is no sun, there
Never has been. Personnel across the street
Just like you, clock-watchers all . . . The last hour
You see that snow, with colder resolve,
Blown into dense emulsion, has printed
A halftone photograph of January.

Tokyo West

Eating out alone, one makes solitude
More remarkable. Better this, I suppose,
Than the day I've spent trying to feel actual
In the absence of a human echo. . . .
I sense a counterpart in the waitress,
In fact, each recognizes each from last year;
Sleeker, less urban then, less desperate,
Maybe, but the same person, one who has
Clearly been suffering the strain of exile.
Hypocrites both, we smile.
"Clear soup and sashimi."
Too bad the décor happens to include fish:
Goldf—calico, really; that don't mind being
On display and gambol like kittens in
The bright tank. Hooked over its edge, a tube
Injects a downward fountain of bubbles

That quickly fall back to a ceiling they
Flute. A westerner in barbaric diving
Costume surveys this world through the grilled
Eye of his helmet. Everybody looks
At everybody. And I wonder what
Detail of my appearance so rivets
His attention, that Japanese, whose hair,
Sheared down to teddy-bear fur, rivets my own.
Enough that I'm alone,
No doubt, or don't look away
Fast enough. Oh, here's the soup—clear as mud.
"I'm sorry, didn't you say bean?" "Never
Mind, I'll have this." So few things ever come
Clear anyway. For example, tonight
At my place I've left on the FM, *mf*;
With no one to hear, is there music or not?

What to make of things? Walking home in fog
And cold, full of beans, raw fish, tea, rubbing
Shoulders with so many of us, exiles
And at home—the fat girl in jeans and leather,

The black policeman, the streetwalkers with
High boots, hopes, and Pompadour hair—I feel
The misery that loves company; which may be
A worldwide motive for swarming in cities.
Assemblage of the homeless, on the move,
Apartment, job, lover, self, everything
Improvised, raw, temporary; and I
Discover how strange it is to work all day
Then dine—no, eat—alone,
Like so many others.
Anonymous, at loose ends, finally
I belong. They swim forward to greet me.

By Firelight. *Die Winterreise*. Death of Henry Hudson

Three heats sting us almost back from numbness:
A skin-tightening fire; glass globes of brandy;
Traumatic dream song in German, which scalds
Like liquid wax from windblown candles, fear
And pity spilling in streams of semitones
Down the staff. For as long as a stylus moves
In in inward spirals, until it stops,
Whatever stillnesses, colds and darks that
Prefigure an end, when by favor of night
The city departs from life, entombing them
In turn, its masters, its captives—for who
Finally controls?—all
This may be put aside.
In fire, fed by my hand, a catalogue goes,
Enameled pictures of what I do not want,
Page after page, curling into crepe; and

Scarcely warms, though with each flash the trembling
People of flame, in spiritous blue, unfurl
Another dawn and another farewell.
You are here; it does no good.
Abandoned to the fogs
And dims of self, Hudson set hopelessly free,
Adrift among the floes of candle ice,

Mountains of gray wave, the vast overhead
Where delirious prophecies play like flames:
Lost dreams of Passage, infernal machine,
A fortress of towers in which the damned
Follow ever-lower spirals to a final
Trough that slowly fills and packs them down in snow.
The coldest of them, crystallized as he is,
Still remembers a former life when two
Drank at a fire, silenced by separate dreams.

Some New Ruins

[On the bomb exploded by FALN terrorists in Fraunces Tavern, New York, January 24, 1975]

Certainly a revolution hardens.
That it should become a museum piece,
Like this tavern, troubles. If this new war
Succeeded, then the ruins would have to be
Rededicated; put on display; then bombed
Again. The dust never settles, finally.
Brokers quoting prices over lunch here,
Heirs of the Founders, forgot their history.
Securities—illusions; yes, and so
Is security under a régime
Where death may be served as the consommé.
Would they have given up wealth—that is power—
If they'd known life depended on it? But
They must have known; and still
It made no difference.
Our births choose us; then our lives; then our deaths.

The past is what has to be exploded,
A message everywhere outstanding. And
Our immediate interest in survivors,
In centenarians, somehow becomes foolish
If awakened by surviving currents
Of feeling, centenary architecture,
Whatever has escaped the empire

Of the new. Guilt by association:
History's suspect right from the start
For having calmly housed injustice, constraint.
Here's what they chose to bomb:
Bricks laid in Flemish bond,
White trim, windows that open; ship-tight build
Of a dwelling drawn on a human scale.
One hellish machine deserves another?
Steel boxes stand all around untouched.

I can't pretend to go along with it.
Death eludes restoration; and the killing
Keeps coming back as the recurrent fact
About them, overshadowing the rest.
An eye for an eye: the future darkens, goes blind.
I I I I—sounds like hammers, building
A barricade of rage. With just causes they
Rush into guilt as toward the state of grace.
It's not really the sadness of ruins
I feel, but rather the fact of mangled
Bodies; bloody rags; something smeared on the walls.
(This is too hot to handle, can't be done,
Or done well. And will make no difference.)
True—though arbitrary and
Abstract; just like justice.
The ambiguities speak for themselves.

Earth: Stone, Brick, Metal

It has the shape of
A boat with the Battery
For prow—and was always in overhaul
As the thresholds and lofts rose and fell,
Then rose higher, harder, until they became
As inevitable as landscape. Now
Embedded in brute stone, a man struggles
To emerge. He does all you do, in greater
Volume; has an anatomy that functions
Much like yours, but for all soul only what

An occasional rare observer lends,
Citizen or outsider; and if you see
Dawn wreathe the city in a mythic
Light, it may be he has appointed you
For this role. There is no helicopter like
The mind's eye, nor any weather better

Than a clear cold winter afternoon, say, to be
Lifted as high as the neutral splendor
Of five hundred high-rises that with frank
Hauteur cleave the North American air.
From the sublime expanse of the bridges
Alone one could die. Human and daily
Tributary pours in from the boroughs,
Dredged up by trains that with sudden magic are
Airborne, over water, afire with cold
Sunlight—before they funnel back into earth.
It rumbles underfoot, a resonance
Of granite, metals, ice. From the gratings
Plumes of steam rise to annihilation
Above the glassy branches of a bare tree
Tossing in the wind's manage; and through these

A glint of distant steel. You are carried forward,
Log in the rapids, jammed at a spillback;
A bus swims from curbside with one sad rider;
Limousines deposit precious cargo
At the Four Seasons; tricolor flags turn
As barber poles over the Museum,
Fountains drained, air sharpened with a stench
Of charcoal and sauerkraut. Sausage-linked coal-scows
Nose down the Hudson, afloat the blinding
Waters of sunset. Laundry flaps in the slums;
And just before dark, the windows ignite; now,
Lamps in bright strings cross the park. The skyline
Is jeweled; cold; like nothing else on earth.
Like nothing else on earth the restless hum
Of this place—a question not yet answered.

APRIL

Awakened before I meant
By soft shocks outside, white wet
Light streaming in at eight or so.
That I carry my daze intact
To the window, where at a remove
Unfocused patches of color float—
Taxis, trucks, early risers—
Things that move and beep and talk,
Each on its comic errand, proves
This a day set apart. But how so?
White petals fallen on the floor.
Time to throw out the dogwood branch.
Think of all the flowers that suffered
And died for me, not deserving it.

Bits of the dream come back:
The Elysian Fields. Yes. Which looked
Like a boulevard, not a meadow.
Theaters. Cafés. Great has-beens
In the fancy dress strained out
From three thousand years of Western Civ.
Silent they stood in poses grave.
It seemed a certain stiffness
Was de rigueur among the dead;
Or they distrusted a body
Who hadn't yet arrived.
"Ages since any of us lived;
Not done now, flesh so outmoded,
Inelegant, opaque." Togaed
In vapor, a gray mirage at last
Spoke four oracular commands:
Travel. Love. Suffer. Work.
"You mean experience, knowledge?"
Know no more than you can do. Though
Knowledge is power, absolute knowledge. . . .
The rest was lost under drum rolls,
A procession headed toward the arch
And flame votive to the Unknown.

Good speechmaking; but, as advice,
It's superfluous, no more than
What I've always done by instinct.
In time you come to balance the more
With the less remote. And compose
A life out of to you plausible
Nouns and verbs; convincing others
As well. Today will make a kind
Of pure, arbitrary sense, then—
Like that blurred array of colored
Patches down there, conjugating
In bright steam, rapidly changing
As thoughts, plans, thoughts about plans.
Occurs to me the city is
A print-out of habit; and small wonder
I belong here with difficulty,
Restless, feverish with those four
Imperatives, navigating
With few instruments, my own
Method none but a mad desire
That everything be near at hand
In a world's monumental fluidity.

Even now five years drop aside
Like scattered documents: the day
Of the solar eclipse, and I
The last through a gate of the park
Where others wait quietly.
At the vacant top of a low
Rise I settle myself on dead
Brown grass for the viewing. The air
Goes yellow-gray, a color western,
Say, twenty years ago. Silence. Little
Breezy cyclones. The day reduced
To poor facsimile. Three figures
Below, aiming a pinholed card
To spotlight crescents on paper—
Something like a burning glass,
But cool, precise, droll.
All of them stand motionless,

In contrapposto, elbows crooked,
Casting ghostly shadows on the earth.
A boy gazes up through a shard
Of smoked glass (dangerous, I've heard),
And the river stumbles southward
In unwonted twilight.
The scared stillness doesn't break.
And notice the grass by magic has
Communicated a wet coolness
To the seat of my pants. Then
It's over. The world wakes up.

A trapezoid of light has shrunk
Toward the window. Without moving.
Things dreamed and done and known:
The record is there that others read,
Notations strewn in my wake,
A language of roadside flowers,
Mostly illegible now to me.
The wasted passion stuns, as a cloud
Might pass across the mind's eye,
The dream of life opaque to life.

Water: City Wildlife and Greenery

The most prolific seem to be imports:
English sparrow, Tree of Heaven,
London plane, and now ginkgo, which
Threatens to take over quite a few streets,
Dioecious, the female letting fall
A rank fruit, yellow globes that rot
And make sidewalks slick and hazardous.
Then, urban dandelion, harpoon leaves,
Mustard buttons coming up through pavement
Cracks, along with crabgrass and plantain . . . .
Times I cut Queen Anne's lace in vacant
Lots and brought it home, where it reigned
For a day and then dropped white snow
On the mirror table. Once or

Twice I brought back some sunflowers;
But they drooped and expired by nightfall.
  Pigeons are more or less a weed
Here, though often handsome in mourning
Plumage, gun-metal and black; also,
Café-au-lait, calico, and newsprint, some
Scarved at the neck with liquid green
Rainbows. Then, the squirrels, mostly gray,
Which keep to the parks and freeze at human
Approach—what is it their tails are asking?
Frightened, they ripple over the grass
And embrace their way up a tree, where
At a safe height they pose as broken-
Off branches.
        At the waterfront
Seagulls, each one uniformed in neat,
Nautical whites, glide and levitate,
Looking like a sort of elastic mobile.
The Hudson yields unpalatable eels
And shad that some people fish for and eat.
Of the common animal species, many
Live in the parks: frogs, a few fish,
Earthworms, beetles, chipmunks, snakes.
And nearly every bird of passage
Has been sighted there at least once.
  The pests include huge foraging rats,
A population of roaches always on the point
Of doubling into infinity, any number
Of mice, and in summer, plagues of flies,
Plus a troubling number of mosquitoes.
There's a special problem with strays—
Ribby dogs and cats that run wild
And live out the fate of any creature
Abandoned to the streets—cold, damp,
Hunger, begging, violence, early death.
Spring gives some relief to this sad business.

Two Parks

Sundays the Park-Fast opposite,
Conglomerate-owned, most likely,
Is empty—until a mother, white,
And a father, black, come with their son,
And a yellow ball and a blue bat
For his first lessons. The father
Wears a cloth cap, maroon T-shirt,
Suspenders, and loose denim pants.
He's tall and stands there, arms
Akimbo, pants flapping in the wind.
The mother tightens the belt
Of her cardigan, buttons the jacket
Of the boy's denim suit. They move
Across the asphalt, over parking spaces
Marked in yellow paint. The lines
And numbers seem to play a part
In the game; but don't, in fact.
Batter up: the man throws, the boy swings,
And—strike one. When the ball bounces
Away, he bounces after it, then stops:
Don't Go in the Street. She
Retrieves the ball, then helps her son
Get a good grip. And, when the man
Throws again, the boy, steadied,
Guided by his mother, connects.

Everything seems absolutely
On the surface today, planar,
The world its own gloss; though still,
I suppose, lit by me from within.
Same wind, same sun, but altogether
Different, three days later. The mixed
Blessing of free hours, a mind that wants
Something to grapple with—which need
Not be rare. An outing then, to that
Museum of seasonal change
That lies between the Metropolitan
And Natural History. . . .

However,
The mood's wrong, the day, who knows why,
Poorly chosen. Too late now. What to do
When the sense vanishes of . . . self?
This from-the-ground perspective
Offers no clues, nothing more
Than a vast general fatality—
As though gravity pressed down harder
On an outstretched body. To have been
Drawn by the lodestar of an absurd,
Unrealistic project . . . Wouldn't
Anyone have been flattened by it?
The historical dimension alone—
Sheer weight of lived lives,
Massed sufferings, crunch of time
Rolling past, cries of those falling before
Its wheels; vanished triumphs; naïve
Dream of all the dead somehow
To have counted, to have prevailed.

The visible facts here by rights
Ought to console: one hundred thousand
Pink cherry blossoms; which, however,
Hang uselessly, of no rescue now.
Time passing, and beneath the tree
A man passes, bearded, with side curls,
In black Orthodox clothes and hat.
Blackness and pinkness go blurred . . . .
Not far away, paired teen-agers, one
Atop the other, lying motionless.
Stunned by light and the new season.
Somewhere children playing war,
Treble savage screams threading
The distance. An idea arcs
Toward me, thrown from the blue:
That, in the long run, life tends
To become a spectator sport.
Is that welcome? On the contrary,
And not to be taken lying down.
More foreground! Zooming in

On pink things, a heavy bumblebee
Bobs, undecided; dangled, it seems,
From a spring everywhere at once.
Putting aside the element
Of fatuity in this, I'm drawn in
A moment by the spinning wheel
Of mere appearances; sunlight;
The all-pervading hum of change;
And how a vast mausoleum, charged
With remains, balances against
An image of blind, of minute,
Indefatigable purpose.

Billie's Blues

Their red lamps make a childlike stab
At decadence. Now and again a hoot
That pretends to know too much. And all
Of us jammed tight together in
The clubbiness of drinking. Gauged pressures
Of a hip, an elbow, mean whatever—
Nothing, or the first step toward
A glance, an appraisal, a mirrored
Interest. Also, a mirror reflects
Shiny bottles and the company behind
One's back: studied nonchalance, arched
Or puzzled brows, flight jackets, scratching
Of a beard. Clichés from the juke box
Suddenly ring true; so that I leave
The bar—and none too steady—for
A corner table a mosquito candle
Beacons me to. There. A relief
To have stopped being after anything.
Who needs it? Besides, one cruises
Mainly to cruise, navigating from island
To island, not counting on landfalls—
Though in fact I met you in a place
Much like this. You. So often
I've thought the word in that upper case

We use for what is one of a kind.
Thought, and sometimes written; wondering
Whether dispensing with names,
An apparent gender, showed, oh,
Cowardice, betrayal; or good sense.
I always wrote to You, supposing
The alert would catch on anyway.
And not wanting to seem a special case
Myself—though who isn't one? Holiday,
For example; with her ambiguous first name.
Nothing vague about the voice, certainly.
Listen: love mixed with a little hate for
Him. Sounds universal to me.

Impression

Brightness of the May five o'clocks;
Chatter of the mob at book
Parties; silver from a ringed hand
Holding a glass; and the shiny new
Patent of a foreign shoe . . .
A hush falls over the dilute
Outdoor evening; men in pale
Linen suits. One more naïve sky
Sent up from Bermuda. Monet
At the Modern: *Ces nymphéas,*
Je les veux perpétuer . . . .
The light in this woman's eye
Clear and tart as quinine soda;
Murmurs and laughter as we push
Into the lobby; the ballet
Is blue and black and white and tense.
A day in the mood of New York:
Cool, rounded, undetailed, in soft
Dull colors. The water trembles
At one's step in a glass vase
Of lilacs. Impersonal clouds.
Starched shirt collar scratches slightly.

Spring and Summer

Only three seasons in this city, really.
There's something French about late May,
Early summer. A stroll down the avenue
Next to the park, under alleys of trees
Heavy with the spring water they've drawn up
Into new leafage; and now breezes lift a branch,
Which falls back into place languidly,
The way you imagine a Renoir model moved—
A slow heavy grace. I'm thinking of green
Lattices, white lattices. . . . Notice how
Even the policeman on his scooter, helmeted,
Goggled with mirror glass, looks dreamy,
Sitting there off duty under an elm tree,
In the green air that smells of water,
Earth, and lindens—mint-fresh, like each
Neatly cut, serrated leaf of the beech
Overhead. A girl in a thin flower-print dress
Goes by. Sunlight in a complex pattern
Falls on her face through the openwork
Brim of her straw hat. Now, an old man
In a half-sleeve cotton shirt, striped blue.
His shortish pants reveal large anklebones,
Sheathed in thin lisle socks. Feelings
Sound like chamber music today: flutes,
Oboes, strings, a piano spattering softly
Into the basin of a fountain....Now
A taxi goes by, with bent celluloid reflections
Of buildings and trees flowing across
The windshield. Fluffy flocks of light
Stir on the pavement. Still, a current
Of pain in all this, like a hot stone
Applied to the chest, weighing down
The proceedings marmoreally. If I
Were to die, let it be on a day like this.
Starting now. And by twilight, as people began
To leave the bars, soothed and rounded by one
Or two drinks, to gather at the theaters
In Lincoln Center, or take a last stroll before

The park got dark and dangerous, I'd begin
To feel it slipping through my fingers
Like fine sand, as everything goes dim, the hum
Of traffic, cries, horns, sirens, a couple
Laughing as they step into an elevator;
The sky complex as a bruise; the sound
Of leaves coming through the window as I go out,
Leaving my city and the people behind.

JULY

Fire: The People

Toplight hammered down by shadowless noon,
A palindrome of midnight, retrograde
From last month's solstice in smoke and flame,
In molten glares from chrome or glass. I feel
Fever from the cars I pass, delirium
Trembling out from the radiators.
The dog-day romance seems to be physical,
As young free lances come into their own,
Sunbrowned, imperial in few clothes,
Heat-struck adulthood a subject to youth
And fitful as traffic, the mind pure jumble
But for that secret overriding voice
Advising and persuading at each crossroads;
The struggle toward freedom to forge a day.

Smoke; flame; oiled, gray-brown air.
Jackhammers and first gear on the avenues;
Stuntmen driving taxicabs; patient, blue,
Hippo aggressiveness of a bus, nudging
Aside the sedans. And the peculiar
Fascination of a row of workshops—
The dark interiors with skylight sunstripes;
A figure walking in slow motion among
Pistons; rough justice of a die cutter;
A helmeted diver, wielding acetylene,
Crouched over some work of sunken treasure
That sparkles gold at a probe from his torch. . . .
Seismic shocks interrupt this dream—a stampede
Of transports flat out to make the light,
Mack truck, Diamond Reo, a nameless tanker,
IiI International, a Seatrain destined
For the Port Authority docks—one more
Corrugated block to pile on the rest,
Red, green, gray, and blue, waiting for a ship
In the Grancolombiana line. . . .
The seagoing city radiates invisibly
Over the world, a documentary sublime.

Lunch hour, even the foods are fast, potluck
In the melting pot: the Italian girl
With a carton of chicken; Puerto Rican folding
A pizza; the black woman with an egg roll;
A crop-headed secretary in round,
Metal spectacles eats plain yogurt (she's
Already mantis thin) and devours glamour
Mags. . . . Our crowd scene, a moving fresco:
But is it really there? The adversary
Today is named Random. How capture all this
Without being taken captive in turn,
Install it as something more than backdrop,
As a necessity, not a sundry?
Suppose just an awareness of the way
Living details might be felt as vision
Is vision, full, all there ever was—this
Instant palindromic noon, the joined hands
Of the clock, end and beginning . . . . Surely
The first to consider imagining stars
Constellations had already done as much,
Just by making some brilliant connections;
Mind crowned itself in a round of leaps from point
To point across the empty stage of night. . . .

*****

Now as a pigeon banks, descends, hovers,
And drops on asphalt with back-thrust wings,
Comes a desire to be lifted in the balance,
Rise to some highest point and then be met
By a fierce new light haloing lashes shatter
Into spears of aurora, naked eye become
Prismatic at last and given to see in kind
All the transformed inhabitants forever go
About their errands, on a new scale: the rainbow
Is the emblem for this moment filtering through
The body's meshwork nerves, and a heartbeat impulse
All around puts troops of feet in step with music,
Persistent, availing, that disregards the frayed
Years, vagaries, downfall among trash, accident,

Loss; or because it knows these rushes upward
On something like heartbreak into the only sky,
Air aspirant with fractioned voices, feverfew
Of the sensed illusion, higher ground, progressions
Sounded in the spheres—so each step takes them further,
Sceptered, into daytime, saluting the outcome.
There is a fire that surpasses the known burning,
Its phoenix center a couple that must be there,
Blast furnace, dynamo, engendering a city,
Phosphor spines that bend and meet to weld, to fuse
As a divining rod—sluicings, spillway, braid,
Chorded basses that set myriad threads afire,
Newborn limbs and reach of the proven tendon now
Let go into empowered brilliance, rayed showers,
The garden regained. In this light the place appears:
Hands that rise or fall, muted gestures of welcome
And good-bye, face that turns and comes forward to claim
A smile latent in the afternoon air, vague crowds
Falling down streets without character toward
An offered covenant—love that gives them each a name.

Sunday Mornings in Harlem

Overcast skies I never welcome.
Time changing hands, right to left,
Rushes forward, upward as smoke,
A cataract on the eye of day.
Cloudy Sundays, our morning walks
Ten summers ago, framed now as by
A jagged hole knocked in the scummed pane
Of the present. We walked despite
The strange color of our faces, stares
From those up or still up at that hour. . . .
A strivers' row: bright brass knocker,
Heavy weight in memory; cedars
In concrete urns flanked a stoop;
Brownstone acanthus and palmates
Mind can still conform. Then, hotboxes,
Some of them gutted and refilled

With garbage. Clouds. The fat air
Sweated. Smoke and fumes. Drew us
On into streets of junk, excelsior.
Ruins. Tumbled ashcans, fluted drums
A broomstick hammered. Somewhere sirens
Whined, and the radio did a tap dance.
Ten pigeons rose in an updraft like flying
Newsprint. A heap of burning trash and tires.
The wino, a conjure, suddenly giant
In profile, let fly a rich curse at who
Passed. Smoke of the past; shoots up
Like carbon into suspension if not
Solution and now flows into the veins
Of a drawing, a tattoo it still hurts to touch.

Declaration, July 4

It enters its second hundredth;
The oldest and still somehow
The newest. Restive sense
Of nationality once again
To be appraised. A birthday at least
Is a holiday—hence their picnics
In Riverside Park, where they come
From hopeless neighborhoods
To cook over charcoal, to laugh
And play catch or Frisbee, all
In the shadow of that Tomb James
Unaccountably "liked" and praised
As a symbol of military might.
Steady expressway whiz of cars nearby.
Grownups, those with the means, have
Left us behind in charge today.
We all but believe something untoward
Might happen—not just mischief.
A true celebration; and that,
Oh, for once we might feel
All of us belonged in the same space,
Company, instead of crowding.

In fact, mischief is the more probable.
If only it took an effective form. . . . .
Seize the city before They came back?
Then suspend all TV transmission
Until the rest of the country
Came to terms? Just kidding, of course.
Passive, dulled, all hang separately
From the branches of government
Among other negotiable leaves.
It still seems grotesquely
Shortsighted: "I've seen the future,
And it's on unemployment."

The future. Who doubts the tomorrows
Of the world are manufactured here?
Differences disaffirmed dwindle day
By day, on every continent.
Distinctions blurred, satellites launched,
Experiments made—the one under way,
Perhaps not noble, will test whether
Society can subsist by law alone,
Without common purpose or myth. Breathless
Hush as we wait for the outcome. To live
The gamble tastes like gall,
Brings one to the revolting point.
Yet the only character of that
At hand is the written; and most of us
Doubt that the legible legislates.
No fun, playing skeleton at the feast;
And sometime again I'll probably
Even run through that little charade
Of stepping into a voting booth
To pull the crank for candidates
Polls pronounce already defunct.

Patriotic? In a way. In my own way.
Asked to celebrate the land (though in fact
No one asks), I would begin with a standard
And for me unavoidable gesture
Toward the landscape, my memories of it.

Then, the people, many of them, and their—
Our—peculiar qualities; even though
With each of these goes a corresponding
Fault. (That most Americans are far
Too sincere ever to learn a foreign language
Proves something.) Qualities, achievements: I
Would single out "accessibility
To experience"; and that wild comic sense
Under which anything at all can be said;
Our inventiveness; willingness to let
Convention lapse when it no longer serves;
Impatience with absurdity, pomp,
And bombast; sticking up for underdogs;
That thread of quietism and plainness
Introduced by certain dissenting settlers,
A formal seriousness surviving here
And there in some people, objects, houses.
I would celebrate the hybrid music
That grew up here, made by the untrained;
And those soft coastal cities—Charleston,
Savannah, New Orleans, San Francisco;
And if not his cons, then Jefferson's prose
And his house; the eccentric, forceful works
Of fine art made here, and the movies
Of the thirties and forties; I would praise
The cosmopolitan receptiveness of this city,
Its countless allusions to an entire world.
And I would celebrate, if I could, the language—
English new-alloyed in the melting pot,
A tool enabling who can use it to build
A city like this one, where superb Beaux-Arts
Temples and libraries stand cheek by jowl with
The native clapboard, International Style,
White Castles, cast-iron, urban high-rise
Vernacular, Prairie School, pizza parlor,
And Greek Revival. For language here is
Federal, eclectic, ad hoc, laissez-faire.
Others will seek substitutes for "nifty,"
"Glitzy," "dumbbell," "drag," "pizzaz," and "cool,"
But I won't. Freedom of speech! For, like all

Dreams, the American, if it prevails,
Will prevail in language; or just vanish.

Also, now that the sun bids fair to set
On our Empire, the picnic done, a world
May be free at last from the American War.
Surely that calls for celebration?
Let all pyrotechnics that can be mustered
Begin: epithets explode in sharp reports,
A long tirade in the grand manner rise
Into heaven like a Roman candle,
Hyperbole on target with bursts of
Brilliance clauses depend from, dying falls
Generous as sundews or thistledowns
That seed the waters with artifact fire;
Then rise again in periods that never flag then do,
Blue night a field for star-spangled banter,
Where red and white verbs shoot lightninglike down,
The air all abrupt with an echo of the old
Oratorical thunder: "We hold these truths
To be self-evident; that all men . . . ."

City Island, Pelham Bay Park

We keep meaning to visit Pelham Manor
But always end up here instead, among
Dried reeds and beer cans, sunbathers, same old
Fishermen; and rowing crews out on the blue
Expanse, "their force contrary to their face"—
Spenser's figure describing the progress
Of June; July he sees as naked, astride
A lion. No lions in sight, but plenty
Of almost naked people. I find myself
Wanting some spiritual analogue;
And say to you I wish some day I could
Put down in words everything passing through
My mind now: alarm over how we all live
Or fail to—dinners out, theaters, sex,
Drink, gossip, Valium and Librium, vertigo. . . .

And how it all blends in with this day, here,
The dried reeds, the rusting cans, anglers. . . .
You're not sure I'm making sense, and besides,
"We are not a Muse." People do the best
They can, you remind me. Agreed. "And yet—
I can't get past the feeling that, almost,
We take a kind of pride in sliding down
That greased track; a proof of sincerity,
Or something like it. Normal? Sensible?
Better off—though that's just what we're fighting.
Long as we're 'young and foolish' we're safe;
Half of that at least we can guarantee,
Fling caution to the winds, ourselves into
The next fiasco—fey, charming, maudit.
An overstatement, yes, and by saying 'we'
I get away with murder. Still. I wish
We knew some other way. You sure you like
Living up to it all? Up to the minute?
I'm not . . . Well, enough. Walk to the beach?"

*

Bare bodies. "Didn't know sun could undress
So many." Smearing all of its members
With baby oil, a Latin family
Flopped in the shade of a striped umbrella.
Radios tuned to different baseball games.
Vendors yelling the sale of pretzels, beer,
And lemon ices. We spread our blanket on sand,
Among discarded pop-tops. Won't stay long.
The burning attraction even of near-
Nudity palls after a while. People
Become what becomes them; eventually
Fate puts our clothes back on. "Oh, by the way,
Aren't we ever going to try and see
Pelham Manor? I have a feeling not."
Something in my voice makes you turn and stare.
Your sunglasses reflect twin umbrellas,
Red and white pinwheels where your eyes should be.
We stare. We wonder why we came back here again.

Summer Vertigo

Twilight ushered in still so late
By the madwoman, barefoot, asking
Anyone for a cigarette.

It is a street of figures
Mostly dressed in white—no one
You know. Or why, when the large dark
Car brakes beside you, a voluminous
Globe of hair, a woman, should
Turn and beam a smile your way,
Cool waves of jazz spilling over
The dash—before that space drives on.

There is simplicity just
In a streetlight and a little joke
In the bottle that rolls aside
From your step. Too many voices,
Too many echoes. Are looking to be
Amused; have forgotten other
Evenings lost in the same search;
Are general and lack subjectivity.

Willfulness takes you underground:
A labyrinth filled with victims, dressed
In several secondhand myths.
To barrel through darkness at 2 or 3 G's,
Venom coursing through the third rail
And poured into the flywheel at a screeeeching
Halt: you do the stations and take the cross
Town shuttle to Grand Central—nothing.
Then, head of a man, body of a bull.
Cold sweat beads the chrome fixtures
Of a virginal urinal. . . .
Back on the tracks. Through asperities
To Astor Place, then to the Bleecker Street
Stop: reborn to the world.

Still the perpetual cruise of cars,
Solitude broken on the wheel of Cadillac
Or Ford. Now, follow a gray form
For a half-dozen blocks, in the rhythm
Of your planless plan; so the night deepens
In a spurious threading of streets,
Though you know your behavior
For thin and strange by the blanket
Disdain of all their stares. The remembered
Ideal of being young and footloose
Comes up and shakes its head:
Bottom-lit mask as a lighter grates,
Flares into life and then dies. . . .

Paisaje de la multitud que vomita—
So much to contemplate,
Head drooping downward, amazed
At how stars billionize in the pavement.
A crack in the concrete
Propels you on to link it up
With an old and fatal dawn.
Ah, there's the madwoman again,
Slumped against the wall, feet
Still bare, and taking a rest
So far denied to you.

Birthday Lunch, August 14

"Some birthdays seem to say more than others."
He listens; waits for the development.
"Just try to brush aside connotations
Of the thirty-third year. Besides, the day
Always loomed large for me; because it was
On my second, V-J Day, actually—"

"When you lost your mother. You told me."

Silence. A dream mushrooms over our heads.
Some birthdays seem to say—I feel the date

Is someone joined to me, speaking, my twin:
Halfway along the road of life Brother
In the middle of a glaring city
Tower by harbor and beacon by bell
For us maybe for everyone birth death
Are joined confused   this morning didn't we
Smile and rage together last of the lather
Washed away to see age there like a wince
Permanently installed   separation
Would be the end of us   married for life
Faithful I follow you into a future
Of ifs our constant backward stare ignores
In reckless service to an extinguished life
We scull reverse toward what we disregard
The golden age is past and a lesser
Time persists the wake widening first white
Then dull then blue   morning gives nothing
But a déjà vu the same light falls on
The unwinding script and you feel yourself
A comet moving out toward aphelion
Zero dark and void where no one is son
Or mother no nor anything at all

"Feel a sense of urgency or crisis?
Maybe. Not just because of the date.
This breakup, for one thing. Seems like, like a—
No, a birthday's just a fact, nothing more.
Risk of flying too high on fancy wings.
A comet, say, if it stays numerical,
Can orbit forever. But let it lose
A sense of proportion, become irregular and
Begin to dream of some brilliant gesture;
Then it gets hauled in on gravity's line,
Swan-song flameout in the diamond air. . . .
Fact is the remedy for bright ideas."
He asks where the striking image came from.
"Oh, out of the blue. Haven't you ever
Noticed how the most trivial and painful
Thoughts play catch? Or how, if we could read them,
Those around us might speak volumes. We tend

To take the smiling cover at face value."
"Facts or not, I see birthdays make you thoughtful."

"Mm, you probably mean long-winded.
It's true I have moods—often mistaken
For morals or philosophy. Granted,
They recur. Just as their opposites do,
Periodically. Do you follow me?"

"Contradiction is what makes things happen?"

"Or not happen. Or just be temporary.
Us, for example. It's over. And still,
There's always the chance we might patch things up,
Isn't there? Isn't there? Guess not. Not as
They were. Sorry, I didn't mean to—"

Much later my double drops in again
For a visit, asks me how my day went.
And if you need me call don't wait until
Next year nights are tough TV leaves you cold
I know be careful let appetite be
The guide now more than thinking or willing
Flashy gestures of the will to be will
End in confusion and self-destruction
Exalted as a form of vital pride
Or honesty exerts a pull on you I
Who better than I can tell ignore it
You chose to communicate and so forfeited
The option of not continuing to be
Dialogue begin that now look outside
See what there is a city a text
For you to compose and revise stay close
To the facts you see there was that moment
Last month when the people and the place were
Just themselves but more bring that back to life
Some time the future will have contained
Your past wait and see among those towers
You may raise up your own even a tower
Of loss does that ring a bell as bell

Or beacon losing has become almost
A lighthouse for us now after ages wasted on
Winning   in perspective is our peace light
By tolling tells us where destruction lies
And shows by shining life is still awake

Bike Ride

I brake to talk to M—on top of his van, installing a skylight in the roof. His straw cap has its own skylight, a green plastic insert in the bill. Green smiles: "Going out to Colorado for a few weeks. You staying here?"

"I'll be out on Long Island the month of September. Really need to get away." We will, we say, see each other in the fall

Condemned, closed to traffic, the West Side Highway has no other riders or joggers today. Weeds grow in the pavement cracks. New York crumbles. MAYOR ANNOUNCES DEFAULT. And if the city collapses, the whole country? And if the country? Possible?

A Sanitation Department incinerator. Conduits dump processed slag into a bin. Smoking, dusty excrement, drawn from every corner of the city and reduced to a common brown denominator. The democracy of waste.

Suppose they just let it slide? A brick wall floats past me, long green vines lashing up and around a window, like passementerie. Just imagine how things will be fifty years after the evacuation. All the buildings smothered in vines; first, a merely apparent erosion of form, cornices, pillars, dissolved under a scaly green cover; two hundred years later, an eerie Chinese landscape of crumbling cliffs lost in leaves and mist. . . .

Battery Park. Castle Clinton restored as a fort for the Bicentennial. Too much of history is military. Why wasn't this restored as Castle Garden, to remind us Jenny Lind could subjugate an entire city, just by singing? Or even as the immigration depot it became later?

Again, military history: a dozen slabs of granite listing all the World War II dead. Arranged in double ranks; with a prospect of Miss Liberty. At the end, a huge bronze eagle clutching a laurel wreath in fierce talons. Aggression, sex, excrement... But here comes the ferry. Looks like a big, professional harmonica—and gives a long toot as it begins to swing around in a crater of water. The sun's a red ball; water, blue, with red highlights.

Where did that hour go? Back on the highway. A few last

secretaries glimpsed through the lower windows of the financial district office buildings. Saving the city or bankrupting it? The big clock across the water says it's late. Time to go back; things to do before I leave town . . . Then, from Governor's Island, a trembling bugle sounds taps. Breath catches. Thoughts of New York during the War. Khaki uniforms. "Skirts." Images from half-memories, from movies or half-remembered movies, swim up. My eyes swim. Why is that. Look, a full moon—greenish, august, fat. Saying goodbye. End of summer.

OCTOBER

Another Year

Driving west on the L.I.E., somewhere in
Outer Queens I pass that trumped-up shot:
A million gravestones, ominously super-
Imposed on a gray, one-substanced Manhattan.
Closer in to the facts, the skyline graph
Shows highs around Wall Street, then dips, then soars,
And drops way down around 100th. . . .
Now, as I cross over from Williamsburg,
A sharpened vista: in the tragic sunset
Each building's half gold, half violet;
Art Deco-inspired chrome-plate towers poise
Motionless in the maritime air and stand
As emblems for that urbane high distilled
In the Jazz Age—one Crash made legendary.
The price of this moment: that it's passing.

Bang! The familiar shock of a downtown street,
Civilization and its discounts, all
Foreground. Either you must look up or just
Abide with what's flatly there opposite.
But how the MOBIL Pegasus images
The gift of wings to words like Then and Now. . . .
Coming back always relives the first time.
Ten falls ago; see me there alone, reading
Some novel in the West End Café, dressed
In black turtleneck, gold-rimmed spectacles,
And French-existential cigarettes.
Staggered by my late New Yorker status. It was
Like a new faith, the litany running
Central Park West, Midtown, Village—New York!
And the whole awful following winter,
Left to my own vices. Nobody cared.

Vast anonymity, at home again.
Free once more to stroll where I'm drawn, hero

Of my own story—as they are of theirs,
Who could have been me, sitting around scarred
Wood tables in recycled clothes, trading bull
About records, this season On and Off
Broadway, their "real prospects for breakthrough
Next month," what's unique about Balanchine,
Where you can get a good egg cream, well-cut
Blue-jeans, or laid. If it's true New York fits
The twenty-to-forty age group best, then
I have close to a decade left to burn here—
Admittedly not with the twenties' hard,
Gin-like flame. Ecstasy? A swelling like
Confidence in my chest. Last year's confusion
And failure, at last, to be solved, repaired!

Orlando Furioso: Sicilian Puppet Theater

A painted flat as houselights dim becomes
North Africa. Palm trees. Moorish loggia.
The Saracen king, turbaned, with forkèd
Beard, reviews his captains, each helmet plumed
Black or white like smoke puffed up from a brain
Burning for revenge. A lengthy speech on
Why Christians are bad. One of the hotheads
Swears, with Eastern selflessness, to die
For Allah and King. A loud thwack of the sword
Against his heart: he means business. (Which isn't
Meant in this little theater tonight.
A dozen or so have pulled themselves away
From more underwritten times to witness
A stagecraft relic. When the old man dies,
The show dies, certainty he must ignore.)
But here comes Orlando, Christendom, a fight!

They fly at each other in a golden crash
Of armor—cuirass, helmet, shield and greaves,
Caroming Dodg'em cars, brass on brass, with
High gestures of valor that leave the dead,
Mostly paynim, heaped up like stacks of lumber.

The winners lumber off, appealingly
Proud; and their clamorous miracle shows
How dolls not four feet tall can be larger
Than life. Orlando, moved by his Maker,
Bodies forth legend in part to reveal
Powers higher than ourselves make us brave.
Do puppets return the master that same cue?
Give him a piece of their older action?
If certainty brings all legends to an end,
A knight is whoever still asks questions?
Orlando, sword aloft, speak: what happens next?

Fifty-Seventh Street and Fifth

Hard-edged buildings; cloudless blue enamel;
Lapidary hours—and that numerous woman,
Put-together, in many a smashing
Suit or dress is somehow what it's, well,
All about. A city designed by *Halston*:
Clean lines, tans, grays, expense; no sentiment.
Off the mirrored boxes the afternoon
Glare fires an instant in her sunglasses
And reflects some of the armored ambition
Controlling deed here; plus the byword
That "only the best really counts." Awful
And awe-inspiring. How hard the task,
Keeping up to the mark: opinions, output,
Presentation—strong on every front. So?
Life is strife, the city says, a theory
That tastes of iron and demands assent.

A big lump of iron that's been magnetized.
All the faces I see are—Believers,
Pilgrims immigrated from fifty states
To discover, to surrender, themselves.
Success. Money. Fame. Insular dreams all,
Begotten of the dream of Manhattan, island
Of the possessed. When a man's tired of New York,
He's tired of life? Or just of possession?

A whirlpool animates the terrific
Streets, violence of our praise, blockbuster
Miracles down every vista, scored by
Accords and discords intrinsic to this air.
Concerted mind performs as the genius
Of place: competition, a trust in facts
And expense. Who loves or works here assumes,
For better or worse, the ground rules. A fate.

Photographs of Old New York

They stare back into an increate future,
Dead stars, burning still. Air how choked with soot
One breathed then, the smudged grays and blacks impressed
In circles around East European eyes,
Top hats, a brougham, the laundry that hung
Like crowds of ghosts over common courtyards.
Dignity still knew how to thrust its hand
Into a waistcoat, bread plaited into shapes
How to dress a window, light under the El
Fall as negative to cast-iron shadows.
Assemble Liberty plate by plate—so
This giant dismembered arm still emerges
From folds of bronze and floats over the heads
Of bearded workmen riveted in place
By an explosion of magnesium they've learned
To endure. Then, Union. Rally. March. Strike.

And still the wretched refugees swarming
Out from Ellis Island, the glittering door,
To prosper or perish. Or both . . .The men
Don't see the women; or see how deftly hems
Can be lifted at curbs—well, any eye would
Be caught by that tilt of hat, profile, bearing.
Others strive to have mattered too, stolid
Forms that blush and crouch over sewing machines,
Haunt the libraries, speak on platforms.
Did they? And did this woman, who clearly still
Speaks no English, her head scarf, say, Russian?

A son stands at her side, crop-haired, in clumpy
Shoes. She stares straight forward, reserved, aware,
Embattled. The deep-set eyes say something
About the emptiness of most wishes; and
About her hopes. She knows the odds are poor.
Or, the odds are zero, counted from here.
The past survives its population
And is unkind. Triumph no more than failure
In the longest run ever fails to fail.
Is that the argument against shuffling,
Dealing, and reshuffling these photographs?
They are not mementos of death alone,
But of life lived variously, avatars
Energy, insight, cruelty took—and love.
Variousness: the great kaleidoscope
Of time, its snowflake pictures, form after
Form, collapsing into the future, hours,
Days, seasons, generations that rise up
And fall like leaves, each one a hand inscribed
With the fragile calligraphy of selfhood;
The human fate given a human face.

Afternoon

Scudding clouds give happenstance to the walls
Of the dome above me. Add the motion
Of my last ride this season—cyclist in all
But winter—add breezes, and what a fluid
Day is rushing by. Though the bike always
Takes me for the same ride, for staying the same,
It changes all the more—not a place but
An event, demolition wrought with speed,
As in our downtown urban renewal.
Whereas the Hudson's a static shimmer;
And seagrasses, reclaiming the landfill,
Still wave as they waved by New Amsterdam,
Fond farewells to the poor stone houses of men,
So jerry-built, so variable, compared
To forms in straw that know how to recur,
And so, last. . . .A helicopter lifts off,

A moment signifies. The wheels randomly
Spin after an impulse and gravitate
Down street names I like: Coenties Slip, Pearl,
Broad, and Water. There: renewal can mean
Repair. Fraunces Tavern has been restored
Like new again, or, rather, old. (Still, I'd
Hesitate to have lunch there.) Renewal:
"Dear Love—We've both changed. On a different
And better basis, we'll be able to. . . ."
St. Paul's bell strikes five and struck the same tone
For the nineteenth century. But I am left
With my text, no less coherent than its day.
Good citizen, discontent as any,
One who has seen home base as enemy
And ally; and lived in contradiction,
The order of this place, in this moment.

The city thinks, but whose thoughts? Wire service,
Museum, financial directorate,
Creator, conscience—mind's the very air
We breathe. Thought by a place, am I that place?
A part of the whole and the whole in part?
These inspired breezes, once-in-a-lifetime clouds,
Pearl-white autumnal light creating suns
Like whirligigs on the water. . . .My bike,
My charger turns toward home. Towers rise
And swell as I come closer, the pedals
I pedal like a pump that pumps them up—
As such, I am the builder. Though what proof
But in saying it, an act, much like love,
That enjoins substance on what comes and goes?
Streets, stay with me. Desire, match with a moment;
See, that there always be one of this day.

Short Story: A Covenant

Together again under the same roof—
Your car's—and we're driving over to Brooklyn.
When patter lulls, I try the radio:

Haydn's *The Seasons*; and, as it happens,
"Autumn." (*Belt Parkway, Flatbush Ave . . .*) Today
Prosiness feels right; so I don't pay much mind
To the unfolding Verrazano Narrows
And its huge bridge. We hit the approach, lift
Off and begin to cruise. The sun tries to set,
Snagged by arch and cable. We're flying over
Water, Haydn crescendos—well, in fact
It's—in spite of myself an impression
Gets foisted off on me. . . . Then, Staten Island,
Which comes as a pleasant anticlimax.
"There's a park. Want to get out a minute?"
We stop. Just as "Winter" is beginning.

Grass. Fallen leaves. Not much to look at.
Thinking about leaves and about my book—
I'm to have the first copy in a few weeks.
"But that's already—past." I explain; you nod.
We reach a bluff that looks out toward the bridge,
The light begins to go, and as we stand there
I ask: "Think we'll manage better this time?"
You say you can't say. We shouldn't predict.
What will be . . ."Oh, look at that!" A wall of fog
Moves up the Narrows. Wind rises. We gape,
And—it's so fast!—the bridge is overtaken,
Completely erased by a featureless
Gray foolhardy gulls as well vanish into.
Fog rolls up around us. We feel chilled, blank.
And nervously dismiss the obvious
Omen. "Aren't you getting cold? Let's go back."
For the return, I suggest, who knows why,
The ferry. First, a leisurely drive past
Sunday-evening streets —Hope Avenue, Prospect,
Sand, Wave, and Victory. There's the ferry.
They flag us into the hold of the *Joseph*
F. Merrell. Which is painted bright orange—
The inside of a pumpkin. "By the way,"
(We're climbing stairs), "what about Thanksgiving?"
You don't know, no special plans. Whatever.
Doors swing wide, we step out on deck. Nothing,

Just water and gray fog. The blank wall. "Cold?
Take my jacket." You don't; but you think
You'll go inside. I want for some reason
To stay out here. Even though there's nothing
To see—well, those disappointed children,
Who wasted their dime on the view-finder.

Wasting time, wasting time. Are we? I'm afraid.
What new bond could hold if the old one broke?
Fog, tell me what *you* think. Nothing, of course,
Or just what I think. You are gray, but no
Matter, just an involved form of the void
I tell myself to; and there is plenty
Of room in an empty thing, all decks cleared,
Ready to be stocked with whatever I choose.
That might be objects of purest fancy:
"Wan water, wandering water weltering,"
Music of a Rhine maiden or W.C.;
Hallucination of the highest spheres,
Myself an orrery for the whole system;
Aeolian harp, Hades, Bower of Bliss,
Whatever. No. Instead of these, bare fact.
My own moment, right now. Here's what we have:

Children, parents, couples of every
Persuasion. Old women wearing scarves, alone.
Men forty, necks weighed down with camera.
Little girls in ties who scream and munch popcorn.
A Chinese man wiping his fogged glasses. . . .
With passing time to be drafted as a kind
Of Chief Executive, my constituents
All of—all of us. But how to begin?
Those promptings. Listen. And thought doubles back
On itself, as before . . . . Your life changes, then
Your mind. A year, a month from now—what? Suppose
We make one more effort; see if we can.
And if it fails, it fails. Go on from there.
A boy sporting a red bandanna dangles
From a ladder, laughing; crying. And we
All make toward engulfment, doomed; and joyful.

Air: The Spirit

Real but departed, like remembered clouds;
As a face seen in water lives and erodes.
Spring days under the locust I look up
And shade my eyes against the sun, dissolved
In a million parentheses, the idea just
To catch my drift by directing a feature
In the tradition of Lumière & Sons.
First, a fantastic silent—moonwalks, love,
Fans flinging roses at the stars; then,
Sound—long rubbery blats of foghorns dubbed
Over our dialogue. An exchange, as
Spirit, in the city, comes to replace
The yes we owe the country earth and to
The earthly contract. For an urban year
The old calendar has to be altered.
Best and last lie upward: a new garden.

In fall, the guest arrived, invisible but
For a skin of leaves plastered on muscled air;
He settled on his back, a sleeping giant.
Leaded outlines against that arctic light:
A steamship, a locomotive, a roadster—
Transport during our jazzed-up twenties.
A thrill invaded the world, and everyone
Plausibly confused the wine of life with wine.
But they couldn't matter to each other in two
Dimensions. Strings hoist my arm and hand
In semaphore gestures across the gulf.
Plural, countless, sand falls in a silken stream,
The sound unreturning except as wind or rain
Trembling through fictive summer leaves. Good-bye
To that stage of things. A black-edged placard says
The world has become manageable again.

THE VARIOUS LIGHT
(1980)

Moving: New York-New Haven Line

Taut on the leash, at last I have my way:
The train jolts off, just for a split-second
Immobilizing a porter I catch sight of
Through my window, pushing his cart. The platform's
A treadmill or a backward rack; for, his feet
Notwithstanding, he grinds into reverse,
Left behind in underground darkness. . . .
That forward-backward prank gets cruelly played
On every car or truck that races with us
Along the paralleling highway; try
As they might, our motion slowly brakes them,
It sends them backsliding faster and faster
Behind; a feeling I recall from nightmares
(Nightmares, and, to tell the truth, from "real life"
As well). Another stunt of overtaking
(Like my own sharp about-face two months back)
Is the fateful rotation a car makes:
Trunk to grill we see it, a slow, pivotal
Display-practiced, in fact, on every near
Item in the window, especially trees,
Their radially branching form flung into perfect
Umbrella turns (clockwise, because I see them
From the train's left side). Indian file they run
And pirouette together, the closest rank
So much quicker than others farther out,
Which fall behind at a desultory pace.

(This constant shuttle between two points has made
At least some aspects of the pattern clearer.)
Passengers riding backwards, though, see things
Otherwise-and must feel guilty about it;
When I turn and catch them looking, their eyes
Drop, and they assume a preoccupied
Air meant to mime some private train of thought.
Impatience? Funk? A half-wish for derailment?
(They don't have *you* waiting for them, smiling. . . .)

Our steady, legato impetus is barred
At regular intervals by metal poles
That fly by in a soon predictable
Tempo, echoed also by the sag and soar
Of highstrung staff lines hanging down between.
I keep looking for groups of eighth-note starlings
To give the gallop a tune, but none are there,
Nor ever even a rest, just a continuing
Inaudible rush, variably elastic
According to our speed, which hums the landscape
Into a final tableau of motion itself—
A thing so strangely still at its utmost—
The factories, ashheaps, stations, transports caught
In a fastness that wants to hold my eyes
In thrall and lock me up in sleepless dreams.
(Your voice is putting accents in the transit,
Pulling me toward you on a silken line—
And dreams that ran   on time   were Vehicles-
For-Something-Else . . . .?)

*

My mind winks on again—yes, there's that river
We cross here now, the same and always different.
A breeze intangible to me suddenly
Wakes the trees and blows on the gray water,
Shriveling the surface into a kind of
Elephant skin. A chevron of migrant geese
Flies into it—bull's eye straight to the heart
Of twenty concentric spreading circles. Water,
Birds, trees, swerve: how is it possible
To be moved in so many ways at once?

*

Our conductor shouts the listened-for station.
Though I've kept to one spot, the place has changed.
That, along with the name, which, red letter by
Reverse red letter, rolls toward me. Our shared
News—and the rest is neither here nor there,

Is anywhere we both shelter, still moving
Toward deeper welcomes, reunions. This racing
Panic will stop, once it's reminded we are
The only place I really want to go.

At the Grave of Wallace Stevens

Cedar Hill Cemetery, 21 March, 1978

"We should die except for death." And even then
We do? The brightness of this early sun's
One light with that other day, five decades now,
When you cleared your throat and took to words again,
Tossing off your metaphysical hurts like
Speech impediments.

The back-and-forth of light and breath wants to,
By tmesis, free contracted hopes in all
Uninsurable things; and let them be
No cause for cause's sake or pieties,
The welling spring, dumb tears, far gone in earth's
Bright particulars.

This simple stone, its ashen pink incised
With simple lilies and your easy name—
And hers, the household tokens you exchanged—
Faces eastward, where Hartford's towers daydream.
A cedar and a budding willow cast
Shadows on the graves

And grass, the last patches of fluent snow
Withdrawing into mud and air; as if
To say, Poverty, be changed to Poetry:
Let the veil be torn away, the weather cleared
For a green metathesis where lucid leaves
Damask this new ground!

Philosopher of one or two ideas,
Touching no strings that hadn't been given—
And all the notions you had had had had
From the first the gaiety of stammered baubles,
As a way to say hiho to blank zero,
Shouting down the void.

These sturdy upright burgher bedsteads with light
And shadow sharply ruled in granite tell
Their legends to a sky *bleu ciel*—a thing
As it is in itself, but translated
Into distanced thought that comes nearer
Rhyming sound with mind;

And clouds freely associating one
Into another, still play to your own
High theater, tropical, boreal,
Informing and deforming what you saw
As final mercy, but, for other eyes,
Less than final loss.

To draw a golden bead on the marginal. . . .
Can you be felt as patient with a bitter
Restorative, a lighter regime building
Ruins to replace what was not at first
Meant for ruin? (Ask, as though you stood in this
Place of numbered stones—

Which might be graves of ancestors in that
Low country of the mind, at the middle height
Of dark, warring with nature's war, Antares
Pendant on the night, the noted vireo
And corydalis weeping over the cold
Spurls of passing time. . . .)

The bluster, the tawny lions of other
Marches take their place in gentle order.
To feel the flaw as a widening melt
And hear the wind speaking along bright strings—
The sun's a hat to be put on and then
Lightly doffed to you.

If it's still right to "like words that sound wrong,"
Take these to sleep on where you rest, under blue
Featherweight shadows, your tireless vigil now
The highway's self-renewing whisper, far
And near: endlessly it keeps revolving what
Time has written down.

November Leaves

Morning finds them silver, quite a killing
At the trees' expense. And, like the delicate milling
That seconds the die-cut dial of a dime,
The cold has etched each margin with shining rime.

Small change—but enough for what there is to buy:
Those white-sale blankets, woolens of the snows
Winter tosses down from its vault of sky.
Green copper silver time grows on trees; and goes.

Two Places in New England

i

Out on the speechless white plain
The snowshoes shush no sound unless their own.
Blue with no ice-clouds silent on high,
Aeronautic blue clear to the pole;
And a polar bloom infuses the fields.

Dry and watered grist, bear the weight.
Keep the record of each cross-hatched step.

A dozen half hoops,
The barbed raspberry canes
Anchored in snow, a wicker the dustiest
Brown rose.
No waxwing or winter wren nimbly stationed
On the stubble's threaded glaze; or on
The thick brakes of underbrush at field edge.
Strawy nearer weeds stand stoic
Over the snow, beside fallen bright berries,
Blooddrops in beaded spoor:
Some dainty velvet pelt, brown by black chevron,
Taken by a hawk, by an ermined owl,
Scripture on wing.

The bare beech, carven and muscular:
At each meeting of limbs a crater
Filled with snow, grails of light.
Will it always be damson bristle on the hills,
The trees and brush galena-bright in sun,
With jaggedly branched white birches singled out
Among them, frozen lightning-bolts
Shot from the ecliptic's great crossbow?

Winter, know, be, and say more than this
Intricate featureless plain of ice,
Shadowed by hemlock,

The needles' tight black plan,
Weeds their own monument,
Seeds their shorthand,
And, on snowslope façades up the rocks,
Scatterings of tiny scythes,
The split beech husks, twisted
Apart, opened, emptied, made past.
Winter, timeless machine, cold presence of the past—
A cold that is polar and blue, in the pastures and snowfields.

ii

The fresh-rinsed rural chrysalis breaks open—
A wing, two wings, trying their fitness to the wind.
The air develops, but not stirs the gravestone,
A motto's Doric, sampler truth,
The marble vigil of a willow standing downcast,
Even in New England, above an antique urn.

Yet we only look and pass.
That a willow would be yellow
All in cascade over the brook
Where wobbling hoses and vocal jellies murmur,
Water; or bluegreen swords have risen,
Equinox germinator, from corms under mud;
And I take this sighting of you
In lost profile against the field—
It comes down to water, and things best made.

Water brought them, the builders and rebuilders—
Threshold to rooftree, shingle or clapboard.
"Trouble to build and rebuild the spring!"
Says the durable warbler coming back:
More subtle homespuns for a nobler nest,
Glovelike, to cradle the fragile prospects in.
Tireless burden of returning
Travelers, skill renewed on veteran wings:
Like a molding made of sound and motion,
Egg-and-dart, egg-and-dart, frames the air.

Naive catkins, pollen-dusted;
Gold of an hour stayed in stacks of forsythia.
Light, be laid like malleable leaf
On polished branches, heraldic buds.

Side by side, across the springy compost,
We find the path again;
Past a broken toadstool circle,
Ghost meats and umber gills, a scattered henge.
Jack-in-the-pulpit back in the shadows
Of a cedar grove is holding forth to show the way—
And what crisper gesture now, spathe and spadix,
Than your green- and white-ribbed flourish?

Here: a rocky seat beside the flood.
At tips of leaves let beads of water-glass
Gather in the terrestrial sphere.
If rivers keep their history,
They keep it silent, all the liquid knowledge
Reworded in one kindly play—
Light on the water, on trees—a face—
To be so chancy, a burden so great—
Letting some things go—that others come—
Taking and giving speech away—the various light.

Remembering Mykenai

Guides urged us, praised us up to the Lion Gate, its
Carved lintel "brought from twenty or possibly
    Two hundred miles away" and wedged in
    Place by the gods or a tyrant's hybris.

High up, the fallen muscular citadel,
Great blocks the winds had modeled and smoothed like the
    Hard flesh of some remembered Argive—
    Vengeful Orestes, the seed of Pelops?

Nearby, the beehive tomb lay, an underground
Dome sunk in gloom. Its resonance chilled us, as
    Trapped flies, whose droning stunned the eardrum,
    Sluggishly spiraled above our comments.

Stones, stone, the life they hewed; and the self a dark
Construct, both tomb and citadel. Why will a
    Dead hour, when change breeds mishap, rise to
    Strike us, metallic and harsh as noonday?

Rocks, thyme, the wind-scorched Peloponnese—to which
Years stretch in mute kilometers back. But those
    Strong measures taken, steps our feet took,
    Echo through ruins like yours, Mykenai.

Tanagra

In that day, even so moderate a ware
As you foreknew that laws like gravity's
Had rippled your stance in streamlike drapery
And fixed your earthen gaze on Theban stars.
Since you were cast to see as sculpture sees,
Change you cannot support you will ignore,
Memento of future but still classic terrors,
The darkening pull down perpetuity.
That myth invoked, assume it as one more
Mantle. Too near to breath to choose the dead,
You help the traveler ford the dream he dreads,
Who stand in fluted robes on modern shores,
A single column, capital your head
That bears the pondered weight of what we are.

AELFRED MEC HEHT GEWYRCAN

Motto on the Alfred Jewel, Ashmolean Museum

Under rock quartz, cloisonné:
Green of a chrysoprase, the blue of lapis;
And the whole encased in gold.
In intricate gold, the scaly dragon's head—
Earless, blunt-muzzled, staring—
Guarding the king's portrait, belling, in Saxon,
"Alfred had me be fashioned."

Ruler in Wessex, the king plucked back London
From the Danes; they'd been the scourge
Brought down on a flock gone astray—its error,
It could not read. The king read
Denmark back into the sea. Boethius,
Augustine's *Soliloquies*,
The *Cura Pastoralis*, in a new tongue.

As justice is a jewel
Alfred ordered the just kingdom: from Northmen
Free, this green province walled round
By blue, its shepherd the scepter and golden
Word—to which he returned then,
"That in the midst of earthly ills he sometimes
Might think of heavenly things."

Prime Minister in Retirement

Is, and has been raining several days.
Dull as rain, our plates of tarnished pewter
Line the walls. The tea—and fine Earl Grey's—
Has cooled inside her cup; it doesn't suit her.

Past, present, they boil down to much the same,
Don't they? Yesterday (and every) we read.
I'd say the future made less sound a claim:
Bonds are promised gold, not gold; and "lead"

In print's no more than scrip until a voice
Or context has determined whether it
Commands or means base metal. Speech is choice—
Home rule. I've made mine and weather it.

CORNWALL

Sun rising at your back,
Cross the dry bed of the Tamar;
Wheels whisking the road behind
Unroll the land like carpet.

No poet, Cornwall?
None to praise the velvet pastures
With hand-hewn cows, couchant
Among purslane, granite and sorrel;

The faraway hillside meadow where
Sheep no bigger than rice grains graze,
Feeding, feeding like aphids
By the blasted pine and stunted oak?

St. Piran, patron of miners,
Come down in the shape of a sea-gull,
Crucified on your trim white wings,
Your halo bright as the top of a tin!

Bless the wolfram dug for treasure
At Castle-an-Dinas, heaped up there
Beside the brick stacks belching forth
Smoke-gouts, a wreath to heaven.

And do you take away the pagan stain
From the dolmens of Mufra and Chun,
The monoliths in the parish
Of charitable St. Buryans?

Best loved of his grandsire Alfred,
Æthelstan took this for England,
He tried to: lengthy Anglo-Saxon
Wrangles in the witenagemot.

"By Pol, Tre and Pen,
You may know the Cornish men."
But not one now will crawl nine times
Against the sun and through a stone

Ring, to be cured of rickets;
And today a boy was broken, died—
Stealing eggs from sea-gull nests,
He fell on the rocks at Falmouth.

And another struck by a black bolt
Flung down through high-tension lines—
Green glass fixtures afire with sun
Climbed recklessly among.

The spiked hawthorns all remember,
Some flushed pink as though with wine,
Blent with the high, savage hedgerows
That cicatrize the fields.

Remember, too, the sturdy inns,
Each with its peruke of thatch—
Trelawney, The Pillars, The Badger,
Smugglers, Three Pilchards, The Sloop—

And the sea-mists that lost to view
One lighthouse in St. Ives Bay.
The holiday-makers paced and paced,
And stared uncomprehendingly

At outdoor trays of turbot, cod,
Conger, dogfish, ray and skate.
(Cornish wrestlers at Agincourt:
And this is the English Riviera.)

Sun declining, but there's still time
To push down to the toe of the county,
Tipping into the Atlantic, O
The cliffs and sea-pinks at Land's End!

No magic if by a trick of light
And cross-hatched waves, the souls
Of the drowned move on the water,
Film-like now in purple shrouds.

They pace, call out, flail their arms
Backward into the deep; and they surely
Have telegrams for long-erased names
Who didn't drown, though will have died.

One changing-color silhouette
Has guessed the shores you left behind;
And knows the course, the sun-road down,
One last anchor in Dingle Bay;
Then out to the edge of the world:
Here There Be Monsters, and your home.

Maine Real Estate

Is hardship renewal? The cold waves
Keep coming in, little restrained
By islands offshore, where they ride
Ringed around by small, stripped-down craft.

Every lookout gazes seaward;
A whole township ignoring the signs
Nailed to walls and porches—a sale,
A July sale on houses. Mist

Rises from the lawns, stalling in the elms;
Shingle slumps, white paint scales, as though
Some genie steamed up from his oil-lamp
Had waved a fist and shouted, Collapse!

Dockside the Maritime Academy's
Grandest classroom sits at anchor,
Drawing an ensign up the gangplank,
His face deadpan, like the face

Of the infantryman a century
At ease on the green, forward inclined,
Granite rifle by his side.
No attention paid. Each citizen

Is visibly minding his business
Even when, reflexively, he
Barks out an "Afternoon"
To others on foot, who nod and pass.

What high, stinging whine gives it away—
That all, the most skeptical,
The most assured, are expecting news?
Word may come with the fog; cocooned

In a morning paper; or brought by the stranger:
Something else that must be borne. . . .
Briny droplets tingle in suspension;
The screen door of the general store

Reliably slams behind the postman,
Who stops, squints, tips back his cap
To catch, where it has broken through,
The pallor of the northern sun.

Grass

At this range, it's really monumental—
Tall spears and tilted spears, most
Blunted by the last mowing.
A few cloverleafs (leaves?)
And infant plantains fight
For their little plot of ground.
Wing-nuts or boomerangs, the maple seeds
Try to and really can't take root.
There's always more going on
Than anyone has the wit to notice:
Look at those black ants, huge,
In their glistening exoskeletons.
Algebraically efficient,
They're dismembering a dragonfly—
Goggle-eyed at being dead
And having its blue-plated fuselage,
Its isinglass, delicately
Leaded wings put in pieces.
When you get right down to it,
The earth's a jungle.
The tough grass grows over and around it all,
A billion green blades, each one
Sharply creased down the spine.
Now that I've gotten up to go,
It's nothing but a green background
With a body-shaped dent left behind.
As the grass stretches and rises,
That will go, too.

September Inscription

R.T.S.L. 1917-1977

We saw the sky descending, gray and white,
And idling oil-black limousines receive
Their passengers, air charged with held-off rain,
The still resisted fall of things that leave.
Studied gaze, to you it would be plain;
But you have taken flight,
Your remnant meaning bared and left to lead
From now a second kind of life. Our own
Persists under noonday clouds where loss is shown
How final words must come to spell as deed.

Pantoum

For Lucretius the sum of Be was Am.

Can they ever come back again,
The late architects of this room?
Am I the clock I say I am
For the day-star climbing toward noon?

The late architects of this room
Rose, instilled with proportioned dream.
For the day-star climbing toward noon
Their gold meanings were the golden mean.

Rose, instilled with proportioned dream,
Whatever flowers will fall in time.
Their gold meanings were the golden mean
To draughtsmen of a well-drawn line.

Whatever flowers will fall in time—
Memphis, Babylon, Athens, Rome.
To draughtsmen of a well-drawn line
Capitals define a mood in stone.

Memphis, Babylon, Athens, Rome—
They can never come back again.
Capitals define a mood in stone.
Am I the clock? I say I am.

Shores

The sun makes a seasonable return.
It photographs the breakers, it captures
What I was and am. I alone here, silent,

Ask this beach to change change into memoir—
Speechless at first, an illuminant that like
The sun makes a seasonable return.

These seeded grasses, stirred by a distant
Earthquake, nod indicative heads to call back
What I was. And am I alone here? Silent

And buried, that earthquake trembles inside me.
Each single grass-stem takes its measure from
The sun and makes a seasonable return.

A stem flexes between root and seed.
I feel the elation, the torsion between
What I was and am. I, alone here, silent,

Acknowledge debts fruition will pay.
The sun makes a seasonable return,
And breath returns. The white waves are breaking
What I was. And I am alone here, speaking.

THE WEST DOOR
(1988)

The Band

Two, sometimes three come without being called.
Strictly breathing, down cool passageways
Where the hangings are (in silk cord,
Fable of the boar hunt) I go toward them.
Each one assumes a foregone expression.

(To have known the struggle'd turn literal
And still fathomed so deep, so free and dark?
I hadn't stopped to choose. But a cloudy voice
Spoke and reminded me that even a human
Face at point-blank range is a cyclops.)

They send me on, bathed in baptismal sweat
At the photographic daybreak—
Abdication more, it seemed, than dismissal.
My nearest chance was to be small, private,
Bold as a child. (Who, eyes lowered, keeps his counsel.)

Naskeag

Once a day the rocks, with little warning—
not much looked for even by the spruce
and fir ever at attention above—
fetch up on these tidal flats and bars.
Large, cratelike rocks, wrapped in kelp;
layer on imprinted layer,
umber to claret to olivegreen,
of scalloped marbling. . . .
Not far along the path of obstacles
and steppingstones considered,
fluid skeins of bladder wrack
lie tufted over the mussel shoals—
the seabed black as a shag's neck,
a half-acre coalfield, but alive.
Recklessly multiple, myriads compact,
the small airtight coffers (in chipped enamel)
are starred over with bonelike barnacles
that crackle and simmer throughout the trek,
gravel-crepitant underfoot.

Evening comes now not with the Evening
Star, but with a breathing fog.
And fog is the element here,
a new term, vast by indefinition,
a vagrant damping of the deep tones
of skies and bars and sea.
Sand, mud, sand, rock: one jagged pool
basining a water invisible
except as quick trembles
over algal weed—itself
half-absent, a virid gel.
Walking means to lose the way
in fog, the eye drawn out to a farther point,
a dark graph on the faint blue inlet watershine;
out to where a heron stands,
stationing its sharp silhouette

against the fogbright dusk.
Then, not to be approached,
lifts off and rows upward, *up*, *up*,
a flexible embracing-forward on the air,
rising out of view
behind an opaque expanse of calcium flame.

The great kelp-dripping rocks,
at random positions,
lost in thought and dematerializing
with the gray hour,
release, indelibly, their pent-up contents.
—Even the scattered feathers here
are petrified, limewhite blades and stony down.
The sky, from eastward, deepens
with the dawning insight
as the seas begin to rise, the flats
slide away, the hulls bear off the ground,
and the eye alien to so self-sufficing
a tidal system turns and takes up how to
retrace the steps that brought it there.

From the United Provinces, 1632-1677

1.
Spinoza in the Hague

Glass of the lens he ground to perfect pitch
Infused his lungs year in, year out; and took
His breath away, and slowed the patient book.
His monument, it stood to Reason, which
Was Revelation for the honest man.
Mastering Latin and Descartes, he lost
The shelter of the fathers' law—almost
His life when that mad rabble who'd killed Jan
De Witt came snarling to his door, *a Jew,*
Oh worse, an atheist. . . . In breathing calm
He waited for the preordained. And knew,
According to his mathematic psalm,
This finite world would not be merely good:
The Infinite had made it *all* He could.

2.
Vermeer of Delft

Very little can be known for certain.
His name plunged deep into his pictures, rooms
That want to tell what muted fable looms
For the voyeur who gently draws a curtain.
The Artist in His Studio, intent
On his shy model, paints her laurel crown,
Blue pinnates against the canvas. Down
Below, his stockings redden and seem to hint
At even-tempered desires. For always She
Is present, keyboard pupil, servant, wife,
Scribbler of heartfelt notes who has scattered sand
To dry her page. . . . As lilting chance has planned,
It covers everything, it glistens—this life
A stream of music and mutability.

The Candlelight Burglary

Open the vacation house after a winter's absence
And always some surface or hidden damage lies in wait—
Which goes to confirm the adage, still not obsolete,
That nothing really ever lasts but Time itself.
This year, it took the form of a second-story man;
Amateur, a detective also amateur would judge
From simple clues: a punched-in glass pane and (power
Was off) quick recourse to a candle-end, abandoned
On the mantel first by host and then by visitor—
This marble-pale wand, guttered, with a black wire
At its core. Wouldn't anyone have thought to bring
A flashlight? Well, a stand-in was near and apropos,
Provided by the absentee. "Through all her kingdoms,
Nature insures herself." True, and someone has to make
An inventory: *landscape with boy angling in rushing*
Stream; music system, more or less new; a chiming clock;
A Federal mirror. . . . Portable, negotiable,
They were what attracted his quick sleights of hand.
(At least the silver knew enough to stay in hiding.)
I'm sure this place was only one of several targets;
And then, effects not used nine months a year, we can
Obviously live without, hence may not have a right to. . . .

But look, now the hindered title, at one stroke,
Breaks free: mine—the law says so—if stolen from me.
(As losses help the gambler own up to what he lacks?)
In each drawer jerked open, a starry splash of marble,
Tears spilled over things taken, or rather those
Left behind for me to try to have and hold. . . . Imagine
The scene in eerie chiaroscuro that sprang into life
For that carpenter ant typing his way across the sill,
Who, how many nights ago, paused, antennae extended
At a blocklike grain of sugar, saw its quartz sparkle
In the glow and waver of invasive light, and then
A distant, crouching prowler, almost giant as his shadow.
A witness so marginal could hardly identify

Or think valuable what was spirited away
On the spread wings of cupidity-with-mind-made-up.
Nor have followed the implications of a psyche's forcing
The issue, fear of discovery, of loss, the curious
Unconsidered spilling of light (and burning wax)
On all that's truly worth having. Worth having, that is,
When we keep, among other uninsurables, our word—
Goods possessed, for the most part, courtesy of darkness,
Which keeps things secret and doing so keeps them.

An Xmas Murder

He sits at the table, cloudlight of March
One tone with his hair, gray-silver on silver.
Midday fare in Vermont is basic enough.
In West Newbury, eggs and toast will do—
Though our doctor's had his sips of wine as well.
"Just don't be fooled. They're not as nice as you
Think they are. Live here a few more winters,
You'll get to know them clearer, and vice-versa."
Three years now, and we're still finding our way;
Newcomers need a guide to show them the ropes,
And he has been explaining township and county
Almost from the sunstruck day we met him
That very first July in this old house.
"I'll cite an instance of community
Spirit at work, North Country justice—
A case I just happened to be involved in.
No, please—all right, if you are having one."
He holds his glass aloft and then lets fall
A silence that has grown familiar to us
From other stories told on other days,
The will to recount building its head of steam.
"Well, now, you have to know about the victim.
His name was Charlie Deudon, no doubt Canuck
Stock some generations back, but he
Nor no one else could tell you—if they cared.
Deudons had been dirt farmers here as long
As anybody knew. They never starved
But never had a dime to spare, either.
Charlie resolved to change the Deudon luck.

And that's just what he did. Or almost did. . . .
He'd graduated two classes ahead of mine;
We knew each other, naturally, but not
On terms of friendship. Fact is, he had no friends,
And only one girlfriend, whom he married
Day after Commencement, June of '32.

And then he set to work and never stopped
Again, until they made him stop for good."
A wisp of a smile, half irony, half
Bereavement plays about his guileless face—
Red cheeks, blue eyes, a beardless Santa Claus;
Whose bag contains (apart from instruments
Of healing) stories, parables and proverbs,
Painkillers, too, for when all else fails.
"What kind of work had all that hard work been?"
"Oh, farming, like his elders, only better.
All the modern improvements, fancy feed
And fertilizers, plus machinery—
He was the first in these parts to milk
His herd in any way but as 'twas done
Since Adam's boys first broke ground with a plow.
And anything machines couldn't handle,
Charlie did himself, from dawn to midnight.
He never wasted a word or spilled a drop
Of milk or drank a drop of beer or liquor.
He was unnatural. *And* he made that farm
Into a showplace, a kind of 4-H model.
He made good money, yes, but not a dollar
Would he spend unnecessarily.
Do you get the picture? They hated him,
The boys that hung around the package store.
The most they ever got from tightfist Charlie
Deudon was a nod out from under his cap.
(His trademark—a baseball cap striped white and red.)
They envied him for getting his hay in first;
And there was more. A boy that he had hired,
By the name of Carroll Giddens, was their buddy.
Likeable fellow, regulation issue,
The sort that knocks back a pint or a fifth
In half a shake and tells off-color stories
Till he's got them choked to death with laughing.
'Course the wisecracks they loved best were those
About poor Charlie and his gold-plated farm.
Just one more case of what's been often said
By commentators on democracy—
How it helps everyone keep modest."

Teasing mischief has crept into his voice.
A self-taught anthropologist as well
As teller of tales, he has other frames
Of reference to place around events
Local or international. He knows
That things can stand for more than what they are;
Indeed, says standing for things is why we're here,
And quotes chapter and verse to prove his point.
"Think of the worldwide scapegoat ritual.
In halfway civilized societies
An animal's the one relieved from life
Duty, am I right? A fellow tribesman
Will do in a pinch, if animals are lacking,
Or if communal fears get screwed too tight. . . .
Anyhow, it was clear that something more
Than common envy stirred up the lynch law.
Their own failure's what they wanted dead."
Seconds pass in silence as he stares
At something—perhaps a knothole in the pine
Floorboard. He looks up, eyebrows raised,
And twirls the glass stem between stubby fingers.
A coil of rope hung on the wall, we see,
Has made him pause and heave reflective sighs.
"Here. Have another. So: was Charlie punished?"
"I'm going to tell you—better me than others.
You see, I was involved—no, no, no,
Not in the deed, Lord, no, just as a witness.
It happened this way—hope you're not squeamish.
Charlie had this boy to help with chores,
The one named Carroll. Married, two kids, I think.
Not too reliable. But so few are;
Nor could you call his wages generous.
His buddies must have stood him drinks, is all
I can say. He'd a skinful half the time—
Was certainly drunk that Christmas Eve morning.
No reason to doubt what Charlie told his wife.
Charlie'd been up to help at six with the milking,
And Carroll, drunk as a fiddler's bitch, was there
Loading a pair of milk cans into the barrow.
He took a slip and the whole business spilled.

Wooden handle clipped him in the side,
And he fell, too, right in the puddle of milk.
And started laughing. Charlie, you can guess,
Didn't join in; he told him to get on home.
'What about the milk?' 'Go home,' he said,
'You're drunk.' 'But what about the milk?' asks Carroll.
'Comes out of next week's paycheck,' Charlie says.
And then the trouble starts, with Carroll swearing
And yelping, till Charlie gives him a little tap
And goes indoors. By then Carroll could tell
The barrow handle had cracked a rib or two.
He drove into town to see his doctor—that
Wasn't me—and word went out that Charlie
Had roughed up his innocent assistant.
That's all they needed, Carroll's friends. *About*
Time that stuck-up bastard got his due,
He's gone too far this time, but we'll show him,
Et cetera. . . . As it was Christmas Eve,
They had the leisure, the liquor, and the rope."
"They hanged him?" "No, that's not our way up here.
The honored custom's to dump them in the river.
You see, the river's New Hampshire all the way
Over to the Vermont side, and thus,
If the victim's still alive when he hits the water,
New Hampshire law enforcement and legal justice
Steps in. It tends to confuse the issue, see?
In wintertime, the river freezes over,
And you can't hope to fish the bodies out
Till the month of March at the earliest.
By then, who knows which state the victim died in?
A trick they've played a hundred years and more
Up in Woodsville, where the bridge is. That's where
The loggers used to go to spend their money
On booze and hookers— who'd arrange for them
To get knocked in the head at the right moment,
And pitched off the bridge into the water.
A famous local industry, but rather
Fallen on hard days by the early fifties,
Just like others more legitimate. . . .
Well, our local rowdies knew the routine,

And, when time came to follow up their threats,
They laid their plans according to tradition.
They knew that Charlie'd have to do the milking
Christmas morning same as every day.
And when he came into the barn to do it,
They'd be waiting for him. And that's what happened."

We strain forward to hear him tell the rest;
The narrative spell is on him, and on us.
His voice weaves through fine-tuned nuances,
With sudden leaps in volume and skittish phrases
That somehow help flesh out what he describes.
We see the sprawling barn across the highway
From the white-columned porch of the old house.
See the barn closed up tight against the cold,
And the blue-gray light of December dawn
As Charlie crosses the road to do his chores.
The roosters shriek their morning alarm, the big
Doors creak open on the darkness—a darkness
Slit with tight-strung wires of light knifing
Through cracks between the boards of the east wall.
Tufts of hay spill from cribs on both sides.
The waiting cattle stir and low as daylight
Breaks in on the darkness. Their master strides
In past the parked pickup truck, his pail,
A battered Rath Blackhawk lard can swinging
At his side, a whistled "Jingle Bells"
His fight song for the working holiday.
He hears the verses harnessed to his whistling,
The tune drawing its text along march tempo:
. . . *it is to ride in a one-horse open sleigh-ay!*
And then all changes. Smash of the blackjack
Against his skull, exploding carnival
Of fire-veined shock that flies to the far corners
Of night. Four assailants leap from the back
Of the truck and lift him partly erect, the quicker
To bind his arms behind and truss them to
His half-bent legs, as you might rope a steer
Or sheep you meant to brand or slaughter.
They take him out to where the car is waiting

And throw him in the trunk like a sack of feed.
Another car drives past but doesn't slow.
The bandits duck and climb inside their own.
Tires screech, the driver slams onto the highway,
A smile and wink all round as they drive north
To Woodsville. The sun is coming up when they
Reach the bridge and stop the car. The lid
Of the trunk's sprung open, its cargo discharged.
He is dragged to the railing, lifted, then heaved over.
The body falls, seeming almost to pause
In air before it hits the water and slides
Below the surface of the floating ice. . . .
Five miles back along the highway, the dark
Barn, the herd, a crushed tin pail, and signs
Of struggle in the dirt wait for someone's
Startled face, back-lit in the doorway,
To see them, then whip aside with a shout of terror.

"He wasn't found until spring thaw; he washed
Ashore just south of Bradford, still tied up
And looking like they'd tarred and feathered him—
Partly decomposed, but not his clothes.
First thing was an autopsy to test if he
Had died by drowning or was dead before
Going under. Conclusion was, he'd died
On land, so as I said, his death belonged
To the Green Mountain State's criminal justice."
"And what about the killers—were they caught?"
"Several suspects found themselves in jail—
And that's where I come in: as star witness.
It happened I was on the road that morning.
Real early. See . . . I'd promised my house guest
Of the night—young Marine on leave—I'd drive
Him back to Lebanon to grab his bus.
I always keep my word, especially
When given in the night hours. Nice boy—
He's been a good friend ever since. We'd said
Good-bye until the next three-day pass.
Well, I was driving home like Merry Christmas.
Into the headlights comes the Deudon farm:

And then I noticed the car. A two-toned Kaiser,
Side of the road, beneath a maple tree.
Didn't know whose it was or why it was there.
I saw one face, Calvin Renfrew's, that's all.
He didn't have wheels so far as I knew.
Occurred to me right then that something might
Be fishy; hut locals never meddle till—
Till it's too late, sometimes. I should have stopped.
They might have banged me on the head, but then—.
Well, even as it is they got revenge.
I'm still alive, however, and mean to stay so."
He laughs a low laugh that would chill the devil. . . .
Then takes up the thread—how when he heard the news
About Charlie's disappearance, he drove down
To tell the state trooper what he'd seen.
"That was the very next day after Christmas.
By nightfall Calvin Renfrew and Norbert Joiner,
The owner of the car (the Kaiser), and two
Associates were in custody. But not
For long. Someone bailed them out, someone
Rich, it had to be, an enemy
Or rival of Charlie's. That's often our way,
You know, to let others fix the person
We secretly hate, then give them secret help
When they get their paws burned in the process.
A lot of people coveted that farm,
However much disparaged it was in public.
When Charlie's widow put it up for auction,
Don't imagine nobody came to bid.
I still see things of his on others' farms.
What didn't surprise me either's how the town,
Lord help me, the whole county took the side
Of those arrested against the murdered man.
They said old Charlie had it coming to him,
Treating his employee that way. Meanwhile,
Carroll had quietly slipped across the border
To Canada; no way to prove that he'd
Hardly been hurt at all. So rumor flew.
If words could put you under ground, why Carroll
Was dead and buried six times over, a martyr

Hounded to his grave by a maniac
Who should have been taken care of years ago.
These are churchgoing people, too, but they
Figure they have a special insight as
To what the Boy Upstairs considers right.
Man is born for sorrow, so we're told,
And some try to make sure he gets a close
Acquaintance with the sorrow that's his due.
Meanwhile, if you can say the things people
Want to hear, then you may lynch at will."
He folds his hands and brings them to his chin.
"The rest of the story you can figure out
Yourself. Their lawyer asked the jury be
Directed by the judge to return a verdict
Of Not Guilty. Motion granted—as never
Before for a capital offense in *this* state.
They'd do it again, don't worry, if the case
Was dear to their concerns. Sounds cynical,
I grant you. . . . But then, you see, they started next,
On me for fingering the guilty parties.
State trooper drops by to ask some questions.
Why was I on the highway that time of morning?
Oh? And who exactly was this friend?
Oh, really? Stayed the night, did he? I see. . . .
A doubt or two'd been raised before already,
Given that I had never married, *and*
Was locally famous for my special hobby.
I'm sure I've told you: I play a little pipe
Organ at church sometimes—I even travel
To play it elsewhere. I know organists
All over New England, and the town gazette
Used always to mention when I went to play
At musicales in other towns and states.
Nobody thought it mattered much beforehand,
But once the tale about the serviceman
Got out, my friends, well, you can just imagine.
Overnight young Dr. Stephens was
As 'musical' as you can be and not
Get tarred and feathered. My patients, some of them,
Began to melt away like ice cream. Stephens,

A local name, respected in these parts,
Became a byword for things we don't discuss.
I wondered whether I should move, of course;
Some rowdy threw a can of paint at the house;
I still get unsigned letters from time to time.
Things must be better where you two come from
But this is where I've always lived, it's what
I know. If I had had the sense to pitch
Someone unpopular from off a bridge
Instead of enjoying music, chances are
I'd be a favorite son. In point of fact,
I've given up the organ, seldom play it
Nowadays. I've got a different hobby—
Your health, gentlemen! No more today, though.
Another call to make this afternoon.
But listen, now: if you'll come up to me
Next week, I'll play some pump organ for you.
I can still do a rousing 'Hornpipe'—the one
By Handel. Tourist attraction hereabouts.
I am fairly confident you won't
Ever have heard it played my way before."
He stands to go, consenting to be ushered
Out under the black trees of late March, down
To where his battered station wagon sits.
Thunder of engines takes him off. . . . But his words
Stay lodged in us like arrows, arrows aimed
As carefully as acupuncture and meant
Somehow to warn or counsel. Not that warnings
In the abstract often help stave off
Particular misfortunes, inevitably
The body of most stories drawn from life.
Misfortunes are the hinges life turns on?
Reprieves as well—along with persons, places,
Passions. A fluent paradox, the realm
Normally termed external, I mean its way
Of overhearing thought and mustering
Fresh evidence. . . . Today, for instance, how
New green on branches and a liquid birdcall
Suffice to announce the chaste approach of spring.

Trout and Mole

1.

Salmo gairdneri, mercurially quick
in a thin silverfoil fish-oilskin slicker,
rash of rainbow raked along the sides,
on a whiplash tack perpetually,
tunneling through a headstream waterwall;
then sinking down to dredge among the drowsing
instars, silt, threaded algae, green-gelled light;
or planing up past clumps and globes of bubbles,
a hovel stuccoed in pearls, absences
come down piecemeal from the Above. . . .
Now something tugs upward toward the flexible, sunfired
ceiling, Something; and so with a will, higher,
a lunge up through warbled mirrorgold
into searing vacuum, brightness invisible,
arcing up to the top of his bent—and snap go
the silver shutters as the wingborne prey
(for once no useless clot of thistledown,
but a crispy bite) ephemerid! is taken.

2.

. . . .down to being a starnose mole, slowly
paddling through its soupy humus (pupa, tuber,
nightcrawler eaten clean through, netted roots,
bones and pebbles clawed aside in the long
swimlike starfirst musing forward,
a darkling process moved through heavy dark);
and in his sighing night deaf to the plight
of graminifers overhead, the dandelion clocks—
O blithe geodesic feather-domes, tropisms, cortex
after electric cortex, feeling the black gnawing
underground and launching forth silk-thread asterids,
light-spirit gliders, one by one, hope against static
hope, the ten-thousand sixteenth notes of Bach's
partitas floated single file along the air, fertile,
always farther, their Garden Psalm, outward into the new. . . .

WILD CARROT

More at home than most, this immigrant
    volunteers a white roadside
hedge—and what handmade lace approaches
    the sparing extravagance
of those kaleidoscopic forms etched
    as on crystal? You'll see them,
snowcapped halves of globe (concave, sometimes,
    like Chinese bowls) and flat disks
damasked solid, or, like buttermilk
    sky, dispersed. . . . Yet all are marked
with blood-dark florets at center ruff,
    King Charles's memento mori.

    It has features in common
with most parsleys (Umbelliferae),
    their intricate, fernlike leaves
and branching taproots ringed like earthworms,
    which, snapped off, smell pungent-sweet.
What's rarity, a matter of few
    numbers? Or strange perfection?
At last, exhausted with the dog days,
    the flowers close up into
tight "birds' nests," bowing to the seasons,
    to earth—where perfection goes
when there is nothing more to perfect.

Assistances

Paris, London, Los Angeles—

men seated restlessly in a room
wait for clipped announcement of a name
grown faint and unfamiliar
to summon them upstairs.

The glare falling like cold enamel
on corked vials of venous blood,
each dyed with a message marked in code;
the dossiers that fatten
week by week, to whispered confidences
from white-clad figures in calm stances
conferring beyond the gauze of a curtain.

I think of you, friend and standard
bearer, first again to set out.
What can you not tell us about
the strong deliverance, the staggered
retreat of sound and sight,
loosing of the cord that bound
you to flesh, whose collapse still kept
a last function, the registry of pain?
Where yours ended, others take up
the relay, its sear and tremble at one
with hands that clasped, with hearts that leapt—
silent injunctions made to those who wait,
balancing between patience and complaint,
until you softly call their name.

Home Thoughts in Winter, 1778

(An ancestor, John Peter Corn, Virginian, native of Albemarle County, served under General Washington, in fact, was one of the ragged band that survived winter at Valley Forge. Earlier, he had been sent out with the quartermaster corps to requisition supplies for the Continental Army. Stopping at the house of a Mr. Parr in Henry County, the young soldier was led out by this landowner's daughter Hannah Elizabeth into an apple orchard. The two gathered a good supply of apples. After the truce John Peter came back to the Parrs and married Hannah Elizabeth.)

Soldier with no rank
Thus am I here
In freezing rains, in snow
And rote inactivity?
Cold, cold, this balked hunger
Blended with woodsmoke
Clinched in creaking
Leather, coined with the ring
Of bridle and harness;
A lifted fetlock
Poises undecided
Then downclops in slush.
Numbed to speechlessness,
Infantrymen articled
To glory mere duty
Mars, waiting half
A war out, musket to shoulder—
O let it say its piece!

Speak and be silent thereafter.
In the end they shall bow,
And nothing then contravene us.
Home to Albemarle on foot,
An easy swing through new wheat
And orchards in flower.
At last, abject, a beggar,
Go plead for her hand.
Dark heaven, does she look
On you now, think of me still?

One goldenrod hour
Among old trees and windfalls,
She reached, turned, and said,
Quietly, "I am Hannah.
Our hopes go with the soldiers.
Here: these are red and sweet.
Others, too, we may gather,
As many as you will."

Letter to Teresa Guiccioli

Missolonghi, March 3, 1824

Pietro's letter will have satisfied you
With the account of our health and safety.
We are tolerably tranquil—and except
An earthquake or two daily—(one of which
Broke the Lambico for filtering the water)
They rock us to and fro a little—things
Are much as when we wrote before. I miss
Last year's travels, the stops at Ithaca
And other places to which the remembrance of
Ulysses and his family are attached.
Of political news we can say but little
As little is actually known—and even that
Partly contradictory. I write in English
As you desired, and I suppose that you
Are as well acquainted with that language
As ever you were. Though I am not there
To speak it to you, I think we must agree
That many an ill encounter has been avoided.
When I call up thoughts of Ravenna—the Count,
Myself and you, as we made our few improvements
On marriage—can there ever have been found
Cavaliere servente as ill-suited
To the role? Here are arrived—English—
Germans—Greeks—bond and free—all kinds
And conditions in short, and all with something
To say to me—so that every day I have
To receive them here or go to find them
In Argostoli. Of the Greeks I can't say much
Hitherto as I should prefer not to speak
Ill of them—however much they do so
Of one another. I suppose despisers
Of Turkish despots will serve as well here
As lovers of Greeks. Messrs. Trelawny
And Browne are in the Morea—where they
Have been well received. Do not imagine
A soldier's grave for me—nor even that

An earthquake in league with the barbarian
Will send me and the Suliotes down
A newly opened path to meet King Minos.
I still hope to see you in Spring—meantime
Entreat you to quiet your apprehensions
And believe me ever your

Amico ed amante in eterno + + + +

N B

P.S. Pietro fell sick, but thanks to the attentions
of Doctor Bruno (whom we have rebaptized Brunetto Latini,
as he is rather pedantic), he is now
returned to a state of good health.

Dublin, the Liberties

Summer, and low clouds hang over the Liberties,
over chimneypots and glistening slates
an echoing carillon of competing changes
rebounds against into attentive skies.

What part of the trouble that Guinness made
was channeled into Lord Iveagh's brick
developments, old benefactions lived in
but ignored or forgotten? Prehistoric
the sniff of burning turf,
an earnest against the drizzle's
brief, underemphatic
scrim that steams over broken walls
where snapdragons volunteer
a red or mustard salvo—
on occasion, the tender valerian,
as mauve as the Sacred Heart.

In shops along The Coombe
faceted crystal and silver candlesticks
wait for those who can find pleasure
in things still useful, things antique;
and houses, for their owners
off at work or gone for supplies—
the dog within dozing on his paws
near scattered envelopes
beneath the letter-drop.

Slender stair rail!
hold up your newel, a small white globe
poised to catch from landing windows
one pearled highlight, and another one:

This sphere makes no forecasts,
offers no hints for future tactics,
but draws into itself each muffled, metronomic

step heard passing on the pavement,
much as to take the pulse of time,
but time not quantified, the one-way push of fact.

Rainclouds shake down tribute
for the Liffey, goods of water
to be trundled gray-green past Wood
and Ormond Quay, the traffic
in opposite direction turning
up Bridge Street right into High,
into the Liberties and the late afternoon.
Driving will be an effortless flick
of horsemanship, deferring almost never
to pedestrians, paired or single, who
make for home (each green or blue door affixed
with a knocker clenched in the bronze
muzzle of a bearded lion).

Dublin 8's promissory brick
is what they know, they have declared for it.
The knocker growls or rattles
as the master of a six-room castle
(not counting cellar and attic)
opens his door to greetings from the dog
and bends down through a backache
to gather bills and letters, hearing the old
wind-up clock plucking its wide-spaced ticks—
plural but otherwise out of number—
from the shadows at the foot of the stairs.

Toward Skellig Michael

In this half-embrace of earth, this
        Pelvic amphitheater
of the Mother, St. Bollin's Well
sends down a brooklet whose chiming
        splash repeats morning office
        to the mist, a slow cowbell
tolling response from time to time—

        wholly spontaneous, like
the gentle collapse of beehive
        huts, their rounded drystone walls
        coaxed by the rough centuries
into simple forgetfulness
of form, a gannet's broken shell
        let fall as the tenant leaves.

Out toward Skellig Michael, the sea
        rises, the foregathering
clouds loose their blue-fringed shawls of rain;
like those that drenched St. Brendan when
        his landfalls along the Ring
        taught one fledgling mariner
how to step his mast and make sail

        for blessed shores to the west. . . .
Here, among stonecrops and smashed cells,
        each tomb's furnished with a door;
        over which, the silhouette
of an ascending seabird or—
a crossbow, is it?—the fine dart
        tensed at musical alert,

        waiting to speed forth from exile.

Stephen Dedalus: Self-Portrait as a Young Man

No. I will describe the arts of flying:
        First the surge, an indrawn sigh,
Familiar windiness of all
        The sunlit death-defying.

        Peak, now sink to hover—
Roads and plots; rivers, beds where they crawl;
        The stink of altitude zero
Propels me up past clouds for cover!

Father of Icarus, claim your right
        To carpenter and be no hero.
But some have shed lost wax sincerely, and I
        Chose the son, who chose flight.

Navidad, St. Nicholas Ave.

An infant quirk of a pine
with aerosol frosting, spangles,
and bulbs that blink red-blue-gold.
Manolito, three days home, they've put

in his picket-fence crib,
paper diaper cinched tight,
eyes squinted in a mask
that looks Chinese or in pain.

Asleep. Trailing sighs and smiles
they tiptoe out to where the Magnavox
screen extolls some *producto*
whose logo's a crystal star.

She glances up at the window
brimming with sodium light.
And, *mira*, snow begins to fall
like manna in the warming air

as from down the avenue a taxi
beeps a brass triad. Then an offended
wail summons mother, father,
todo el mundo back to his side.

New Year

Another year, another return—
Each one has drawn closer to home.
A perennial naïf, whose pleased
intake of breath is meant to welcome
back the urban crush, prefers

familiar brickfronts and squares
even to vistas down the proud
colonnades and quays of Paris,
mountains lost among high clouds,
or domes at dawn in the pastel east.

These westward windows, fifteenth floor,
make a triptych frame for sunset—
which shows the buildings as somehow
more thoughtful than they often get
described as being; while the sky,

with blue impartiality,
may be forecasting the first
snowfall. . . . To sense purpose in turning
to the desk again seems right,
the crossed-out sentences and lines

summoning words and pauses always
nearer those that will be felt
as having stood by from the start,
waiting to assume their place.
The heat clicks on. Somewhere a bell.

All the objects here have twinned themselves
with stories. The room's a cradle, or an ark;
it says that half the point of our departure
is coming back—suggestion followed by one
who breaks off work to watch the setting sun.

AUTOBIOGRAPHIES
(1992)

A Village Walk Under Snow

Roiling flakes,
The lunge of a million carousels
In free fall makes
Frame houses' old pastels

By contrast bright
As fresh enamel: while that Ford
(In negative white)
Reveals the silkenly scored

Streamlines wind
Tunnels were designed to test.
Cold weather, friend,
Truest if not the best,

Is seeing saving—
This tufted pine branch, thick with spume
As a poised shaving
Brush or egret's plume,

Mine to keep?
And those post-Xmas Xmas trees
Fallen asleep
In snow and left to freeze

On kelp-strewn sands of
The vacant public beach. . . .Enough
That wheeling bands of
Gulls patrol a rough-

Hewn, bile-dark sea,
Rising to meet the falling sky
Where gulls are free,
Hovering, to dive or cry.

(A bold one dives
Right now, just past my head—one more
Of those close shaves
Outdoors is noted for.)

Jumbo lace,
A complex tire-track hems the path
My steps retrace
In the homeward aftermath—

Gray skies, bare trees,
Houses seen through veils of snow,
Affording ease
Good for an hour or so.

Cannot Be a Tourist

Not casually. Within two days
Streets and vista are mine forever,
Some last few wisps of jet lag clearing
As senses expand to occupy
A space already second nature.

How many facts, though, work against
Staying put. A rented house;
An unknown language stumbled over;
Formal obligations, debts,
In taut suspense back where we vote.

Brought home so often, still the dried
Pages of the journal are more
Compelling than they have a right,
Much reasonable right, to be.
Only alight on them and now

Ancestor olives near Delphi
Stand in an oddly youthful trance;
The vines outside Siena, leaf
By jagged, gold-veined, classic leaf,
Outline the sun in a dust of earth;

Bronze, coal-green, the Haitian bantam
Stalks a wall spilled over with red
Bougainvillea; or Quai Voltaire's
Streaked pediment enshrines a crush
Of half-nude marble, artist-cohorts

Living it up in their garret (the Seine
By night, each lamp secreted in oyster
Mist). . . .Facts be damned: some part follows
Hereafter and continues. At home
Where the heart enlarged by affection is.
Whoever could not be a tourist

Shuts the door pro forma only—
Aware, even so, that form's good practice
For firm conclusions, holding steady
When time says, "Bid the earth farewell."

La Madeleine

1.

Posters of Juliette Greco, the Eiffel
Tower. A good French bistro in the Village,
Its cuisine by some oversight not yet
Widely known; all the more murmured over
By our party of four avid diners,
Leaning forward over the red-checked cloth.
First course dispatched in record time, I could
Be more deliberate with the second.
Enough to admire each tender forkful
Or the fragrant *Coquille St. Jacques,* steaming
In its ribbed scallop shell—eyes even so
Straying to glance at plates on either side.
In fact, we all sampled each other's entrée
And, satisfied, returned to our first choice.
When time came to moan at the dessert list,
Among the dazzlements our friend Richard,
The translator of Proust, saw handwritten
Copperplate flourishes near the bottom
Propose "Compote de Fraises avec Madeleines."
In lieu of some duller, full-dress homage,
We had them brought for all of us, berries
In red syrup, plus moist, butter-and-egg
Cakes, fluted backs golden by candlelight.
Why *don't* they call these little scallop shells
"Les biscuits St. Jacques"? No, another more
Romantic saint has given them her name.
(Mary Magdalene's the revered object
Of pilgrimages as well, her grotto
In Provence—but let's postpone that visit.)

My story over coffee
Began with a concert given at La Madeleine,
The church disguised as a svelte Greek temple,
Where Parisians rich or devout or both at once
Come to see and be seen or, who knows, seek
Forgiveness for sins like self-righteousness.

Still queasy from a three-hour lunch, never mind,
I'd bought my ticket, let music be the tonic
For day-of-arrival hyperactivity. . . .
Ushers were all women of the congregation,
Older, *soignées*, managing subtly to convey
The impression that each was the finer, calmer
Outcome of a worldly personal history now
Put aside in favor of good works and some ideal
Of repose. The one who seated me, gray silk jacket
Over pleated mauve *charmeuse*, smiled and gravely
Searched my eyes as I did hers, both of us refreshed,
I think, poised at ready for an hour of colliding
Gold reverberations, courtesy of Gabrieli. . . .
A week later in a ward of the American Hospital
I saw that same devout double of Jeanne Moreau
Making what looked like a round of volunteer
Visits to the dying—one of them a friend
I'd come to see. The image surviving, framed
Against starched white bedclothes, is a dark profile
Bent slightly forward as she takes the elderly,
Mottled hand of a patient, his health now broken,
Yet only a year ago young and strong and immune.

2.

Proust would have been a *flâneur* in La Madeleine,
Along with how many prototypes of Odette de Crécy.
And what did he know about its patroness?
A few paintings from the Louvre or Venice,
Namesake heroines in Balzac and Fromentin,
Plus his own in the story *L'Indifférent*. . . .I
Remember from a visit to Galilee (four years
Now) on our drive north along the bluegreen lake,
A signpost marked MIGDAL (in Hebrew: "tower").
That must have been, seventy generations back,
The place of origin of Saint Mary, Jesus's friend,
The only woman that might count as a disciple
And first to recognize, according to St. John,
Her risen Lord. Whether as well the suppliant
Who wept at Jesus's feet and dried them with her hair,

Sumptuous, "a great sinner," with gold to spend
For an alabaster vase of fragrant spikenard—
Well, tradition's the richer for having thought so.
Because of their devotion, Mary of Magdala
And the Beloved Disciple in time emerged
As closest to his heart—with iconic appeal as well,
To judge by Renaissance art and its aftermath.
"Let him who is without sin cast the first stone at her."
Weakness of the flesh was routine, so decreed
The late Church fathers as the taxonomy
Of transgression was being drafted. Witness
Paolo and Francesca, lovers whose misdeed
Weighed just enough to earn them a fiery nest
At the whirlwind's heart in upper Inferno—
And perpetual fame in the Testament of Beauty.

3.

You were one of those four at dinner, remember?
Any candlelit meal by extension also serves
To celebrate years of settled union. The lens
Of the mind's eye is I guess appropriately
Vaselined by time so that scenes from the life
Return in a tender, peach-toned soft-focus,
Happy years? Yes, at first. Afterwards, four or five
Spent *together* at least, trying to remember
Happiness is only one kind of fulfillment.
A riddle to imagine how you see us now—
But then, I never knew, not even in the early days,
Before you came to see larks and sparks (Parents,
Avoid them) as betrayal pure and simple.
Thinking of you intent on *Pelléas* (Act III:
Mélisande leans from a tower window and lets
Yards of golden hair cascade over her lover),
Your right hand aloft and darting, to assist
The maestro; or tickled by a page in Colette;
Or quoting an Auden line that seemed to hold
All wisdom, who wouldn't assume words and music
Had some point for you in mere experience,
Were more than self-enclosed palaces of art,

In fact, offered shelter and counsel even to us
With our grouches, gourmandise, and dirty socks?
No? On conduct taken for granted in Bloomsbury
Or Montmartre down came a gavel termed *Love.*
The daze of seeing you doubt I did, the jolt
Of hearing instinct or impulse interpreted
As callousness aforethought—one more lesson
In the power of words, nothing like clock hands
Unfailingly recycled to the harmless
Hour before what was said was said . . . Two years along,
I can see, though, that time is absolution, and many
Rehearsals have now sublimed the old debate
Into light breezes like those the opera chorus
Irresistibly wafted into the key of F major,
Or like a barcarolle, a waltz, a cradle song—
"Lay your sleeping head, my love, human. . . ."

4.

Faceless harm, invasions up from the id,
That underworld mined with caverns accessible
Only through the Gate of Horn, or the maudlin
Inarticulation that overflows censorship
When we stretch out for today's analysis
In the position of love and sleep and death.
Where does the violence come from, and who
Is being killed. . .. The undeterred cast a stone,
And another and another, heaping a rubble cairn
Over the buried victim's blood-soaked clothes,
That fossilized taboos, appearances, the will
Of the majority, this time also be enforced.

5.

Those travels in the provinces,
Up mountain to Vézelay;
Or underground in Lascaux
To trace vestiges left
By a social unit clothed

In half-cured pelts of a mammal
Cousin at many removes,
First effort to draw a fine
Distinction between the human
And the animal. Outlines
Of aurochs, stag, and ibex
In soot or manganese
Dredge up iconic imprints
Of internal prehistory—
Attraction and disgust
At the torch of a furred flank,
Perceived at once as foe
And bloodhot, maternal
Source of nourishment.
Would the stag at last forgive us
For bringing him down with a spear,
And send us more of his kind
In seasons to come? Only
If we kept his image alive
In a vault deep underground,
Where he ranged for humid aeons
Among four-legged fellows
At ease in the limestone fields
Enclosing a pitch darkness
Now and then broken when swaying
Torchlights rounded a veer
In the cave (distant, inverse
Forebear of the highrise),
Like a long chain of molten
Gold, to bring new cravings,
Forms, propitiations,
To hallowed flocks already
Portrayed by an earlier art,
Memorial of what's called
(After the cave's first name)
The Magdalenian culture.

A pause here before I forget
(Sympathy for the waiter
With several plates on his arm)
To mention Sainte-Baume, Mary's

Hermitage late in life.
Golden legend recounts
How with Martha and Lazarus
She sailed to Gaul, arriving
At Roman Marsilia,
Where (the spirit's wings
Widespread) she preached in *koine*
To listening multitudes
Of stolid barbarians—
And, years after, withdrew
To a hillside cave near Aix,
Her final days told out
In prayerful penitence,
Itself the fragrant balm
Preparing her body for death.
Today's visitor enters
A humid darkness, the rough
Stone floor cratered with puddles
Reflecting liquid shards
Of larkspur blue and scarlet
From stained-glass ogive windows.

In cool silence you may
Say a prayer to the saint,
Rise and find a path
Through trembling, jewel-like water,
Pause at the door to look back—
Then exit into the whitehot
Sun towering over the Midi.

6.

Feast of St. James, 1989

Dear David, Happy fifty-sixth birthday. Shall I
This time write (as I daily think of you)
And allow friendship to go on evolving—
In some ways more evenhanded than back
When you were with us, subject to wincing
Stresses the temple of the body has to bear,

Hunger pangs, noise, fatigue, bronchitis.
The week of your death, along Village sidewalks
Linden flowers dusted the air with the faint
Potpourri that will now always summon up,
In bouts of silent thought, our own *belle époque*. . . .

At any dinner party the best finale was you.
A compote of phrases derived from native wit
And close readings of the Elizabethans,
James, Yeats, Stevens, and *The Remembrance*.
Involuntary allusion smiles and sees you
As a second Charles Swann, relaxed and upright
In a *traghetto* as you skimmed across the Canal
Under the shadow of Santa Maria della Salute
To lend some luster to a gathering where,
Apparently, simply leaning against a door,
Arms folded, face lit by an amused, benign
Expression, could magnetize them to your side,
Eager for smiling urbanity's angle on whatever
Venice might be buzzing about that given day.
You had (outside *Swan Lake*) no single Odette,
Rather, a series, cygnet after black and white
Cygnet, whom with a twinkle you brought to parties
(Depending) or skipped parties to stay home with. . . .
Memory's parenthetical invasions of the daily
Round promise to keep you now and future decades
The faithful companion of my "decrepit age,"
As Yeats ("The Tower") called the rest of his climb.

Venice from time immemorial beset by plagues,
No surprise should the palazzo's proprietress,
Hearing of your condition, panic and with all
The innocence of misinformation have your floor
Fumigated, clouds of tear-gas mingling with those
In the library ceiling's frescoes. . . .When you turned
For a last look at the Barbaro (before the long
"Wreck of body, slow decay of blood"), slimegreen
Waves at work to dissolve how many surrounding
Morose or fanciful façades, over the Mahlerian rush
Of waters and motors, bells tolling from the distant
Campanile, dialect outcries, adagio strings

Wafting across the Canal, was there also, if heard
Only in the inner ear, a faintly beating sibilance,
Descending, settling to rest, the wings of the dove?

7.

LA MADDALENA

The baroque streetwalker Caravaggio painted,
His contemporary, a piece of cake from Trastevere
In Fortuny brocade, slumped in a chair next cast-off
Finery, serpentine chains of massive gold,
A broken string of pearls, vial of fragrant oil
She can no longer pour over the Master's head
And anoint him king. Head bowed, auburn hair
Streaming over her shoulders, behold a type
Of the unfaithful, returned from the fleshpots,
Agonized and with no intimation that dawning
Day in a garden outside the city will find her
Weeping by the tomb ("Elle a pleuré comme
Une Madeleine," as older women used to say),
Only to hear her name and answer, "Rabboni!"
Then be commanded to go and tell the brothers,
Her "I have seen the Lord!" echoing down
Twenty centuries in the breaking of the bread—
Whenever broken "for the remembrance of me."

8.

Feast of St. Mary Magdalene, 1990

Mary of Magdala,
Vividest apostle,
Teach me to be faithful;
And to discount mistakes
Others may have made
Out of pain and confusion.
Pray for the sick, the dying,
And those who watch at their side.
Help us to dry our tears;

Or, if they will not cease,
Then let them bathe the feet
Of our best advocate.

At each new step of the stair,
Blessed Mary, pray for us—
And remember us on that day.

Contemporary Culture and the Letter "K"

First inroads were made in our 19-aughts
(Foreshadowed during the last century by nothing
More central than "Kubla Khan," Kipling, Greek
Letter societies, including the grotesque KKK—
Plus the kiwi, koala, and kookaburra from Down Under)
When certain women applied to their moist eyelids
A substance pronounced *coal* but spelled *kohl*,
Much of the effect captured on Kodak film
With results on and off camera now notorious.
They were followed and sometimes chased by a platoon
Of helmeted cutups styled the *Keystone Kops*, who'd
Freeze in the balletic pose of the letter itself.
Left arm on hip, leg pointed back at an angle,
Waiting under klieg lights next a worried kiosk
To put the kibosh on Knickerbocker misbehavior.
Long gone, they couldn't help when that hirsute royal
King Kong arrived to make a desperate last stand,
Clinging from the Empire State, swatting at biplanes,
Fay Wray fainting away in his leathern palm
As in the grip of African might. Next, marketing
Stepped up with menthol tobacco and the brand name
Kool, smoked presumably by models and archetypes
Superior in every way to Jukes and Kallikaks.
By then the race was on, if only because
Of German *Kultur*'s increasing newsworthiness
On the international front. The nation that had canned
Its Kaiser went on to sponsor debuts for the hero
Of *Mein Kampf*, Wotan of his day, launching thunderbolts
And Stukas, along with a new social order astonishing
In its industrial efficiency. His annexing
Of Bohemia cannot have been spurred by reflecting
That after all Prague had sheltered the creator
And in some sense alter-ego of Josef K.,
Whose trial remained a local fact until the fall
Of the Empire of a Thousand Years, unheard of in "Amerika"
Of the Jazz Age. But musicians Bix Beiderbecke and Duke
Ellington somehow always took care to include the token

Grapheme in their names, for which precaution fans
Of certain priceless '78s can only be grateful.
They skipped and rippled through a long post-war glow
Still luminous in the memory of whoever recalls
Krazy Kat, Kleenex, Deborah Kerr, Korea, Kool-Aid,
And Jack Kennedy. Small wonder if New York had
A special feeling for the theme, considering radical
Innovations of De Kooning, Kline, and Rothko. This last
Can remind us that bearers of the letter often suffered
Bereavement and despair (cf. Chester Kallman) and even,
As with Weldon Kees, self-slaying. Impossible not to see
Symptoms of a malaise more widespread still in a culture
That collects kitsch and Krugerrands, with a just-kids lifestyle
Whose central shrine is the shopping mall—K-Mart, hail to thee!
To "Kuntry Kitchen," "Kanine Kennels," and a host of other
Kreative misspellings kreeping through the korpus
Of kontemporary lingo like an illness someone someday
(The trespass of metaphor) is going to spell "kancer."

True, there have been recidivists in opposite
Direction (a falling away perhaps from the Platonic ideal
Of *tò kalón*[1]) like "calisthenics" and Maria Callas,
Who seem to have preferred the less marblelike romance
Of traditional English. This and related factors make all
Supporters of the letter "k" in legitimate forms
And avatars cherish it with fiery intensity—
All the more when besieged by forces beyond
Anyone's control, at least, with social or medical
Remedies now available. Dr. Kaposi named it,
That sarcoma earmarking a mortal syndrome thus far
Incurable and spreading overland like acid rain.
A sense of helplessness is not in the repertory
Of our national consciousness, we have no aptitude
For standing by as chill winds rise, the shadows gather,
And gray light glides into the room where a seated figure
Has taken up his post by the window, facing away from us,
No longer bothering to speak, his mind at one with whatever
Is beyond the ordinary spell of language, whatever dreams us
Into that placeless place, its nearest image a cloudless
Sky at dusk, just before the slow ascent of the moon.

---

[1] *tò kalón*: Greek, "the beautiful"

The Jaunt

In party outfits, two by two or one by one
(I was expected to go along as well),
They step up the steep gangplank, hands on
Metal railing. The river, youthful also
In midnight blue with sunset-tinted wavelets,
Lets them borrow its broad back
For an evening's unhurried round trip,
Which won't interrupt old river habits for long.
Not the chop and churn of big propellers
As the rocking stern heaves off and wheels fanwise
Into the current, nor a short blast from the stack,
Not the up-tempo drumbeat of the black-tie combo
Nor an answering fusillade of popped corks, not geysers
Of laughter pitched flagpole high among flailing
Limbs out on the polished floor nor the mixed
Babble of sideline comment over bubbling glasses
Can shake that seamless imperturbability. . . .

When the springy net of sparkles has shrunk and faded
Out of sight, the last rough throb been coaxed
From the tenor sax's frog-in-the-throat, the final
Needling tremolo of the clarinet been wrapped up
In distance, suddenly it is strange to be here
In lilac afterglow with trout-leap and mayfly. . ..
Strange, too, how our part of the river continues
To trundle along its tonnages of water and motion.

The unused ticket spins to the ground.
As much as any person not two people can
I miss the jaunt, for just this one hour of dusk. . . .
Then, a veiled echo, my name called as I turn
To answer, eyes adjusting to where we are
At the pivot of night, the cusp of light.
Light enough to feel our way back to the grove
Of alders along the curving path beside the river;
Light enough to recognize my life when I see it,
Going in its direction, more or less at the same pace.

PRESENT
(1997)

THE SHOUTERS

A fiercer form of homelessness, an exile
From the brisk release that conversation offers:
You've heard them on the street, snapped to alert
As they barked cusswords at—what? some blood-red
Ghost that loomed and stalked as you approached.

That sweeping hand, as though it held a gavel,
Flung down a tattered gauntlet or was aiming
Karate chops at an invisible
Assailant, adds the punch of blunt conviction
To words that pump white steam into the cold.

Common explanations, whether hormonal
Failure (aging women diagnostic
Victims of that), schizophrenia, booze,
Downtown attitude or bigotry,
Don't quite account for voices raw as theirs.

What makes you stop and see this one as crowned
With a halo of syringes, each injecting
Various doses of addictive damage
Since childhood, when a parent screamed "*Shut up*,"
Or the year love crashed down around his head, or—

"Shut *up*!" he shouts (as others have) and shudders
Enough to block overtures always worth
Risking . . . unless it's clear a mind divided
Is getting back at itself and will go on
To heights where the air burns thin and it can shout
And shout until encroaching silence falls—
Sheltered up there, where all our cries are heard.

Lago di Como: *The Cypresses*

Cupressus lusitanica,
The species name, and factual
Probes in an old *Britannica*
Confirm it came from Portugal.

Greeks, too, arrived as immigrants
And planted the olive at its side,
A Mediterranean romance
Green long after Greek had died.

The drawback? Immobility,
But isn't the breezes' clear intention
To set the rooted captives free
With four fresh knots of intervention?—

Which bends them in a flexible arc
As buried souls wake up again,
Fresh conscripts drawn out of the dark.
Tall, tapering, and midnight green,

They stand as cypress did for them,
Anonymous memorials
Disburdened of the flat pro tem,
In soil thought through by human skulls.

When the trees stir and tremble (much
As their Lisbon cousins might have done
In the great earthquake), only a Dutch
Painter would try to render one.

I'm satisfied to watch as light
Begins to slant and breezes fall.
In shade as dark as minor night,
They hear my tentative footfall,

And breathe a welcome neither Greek
Nor Portuguese, a country drawl,
Seasoned without being antique:
"Come join these ranks for the long haul!

Of course there is an alternative
Less obstinate than our endeavor,
Which only suits those who can give
Notice to time and change forever."

In the distance I see a small van go
Speeding away with passengers,
Who might say "We're not ready," though
What happens happens when *it* prefers.

Becalmed a moment, the trees will soon
Return to their colloquium,
Branches billowing toward the moon
Risen over Elysium.

Little Erie Railroad

In the North, in December, a costly Christmas toy
Cleaves a path through drifts of crystallized
Ether, and spruces shaped like spruce cones dot
White hills around the track (elliptical,
Bemused, a forward ladder with no conclusion,
Its parallelling rails in polished silver
Deftly stapled to fragrant redwood sleepers).

Vibrations and a distant fife note signal
The golden locomotive's precise and long
Awaited advent, transport swelling closer
Like a thrown discus, do you see the wheels
Cycling in tandem, dynamic, dynamic, dynamic,
"I *am* here. . . ." But then its streamlines erase themselves,
Banner headline of the high whistle sidling

A half step down in pitch as caboose dwindles
To a crimson fleck, fine tingles in the track
Sole proof our fleet forsaker was ever here.
Wait. It has stopped. A spout from the water tank
Dips down to kiss the intake, which swallows
A braid of ice water. Meanwhile puffballs
Of angel hair are huffed aloft from the stack.

There. It's done, the conduit withdrawn, a forward
Jolt, and they're off to the races, with a hoot
Echoing through tunnels swiftly negotiated,
Slung coda of cars in mother-of-pearl and vermeil
Snaking along behind when it slows for the curve
Then bends into the next straightaway as snow
And evergreens whizz into blurred bands of color.

To locate its motives you'd have to pry open
The fire door, whose hinges give a tiny shriek
Of merriment at spoonfuls of proffered coal,
Each separate lump inscribed with fossil fern.
The furnace within burns blueish white, where flame
Is frozen vapor at absolute zero, converting
Burnt fuels into variable speeds around

The circuit. Miles to go, and the sleepers groan
When its oily golden belly passes over them.
At nightfall, a tiny carbide headlight flicks on,
Projector's beam hurled onward into a moonless *film noir*,
Adding what seems like conjuration to impromptu
Salvoes of constellated fireworks—no doubt
Even more touching seen from a certain distance.

Sugar Cane

Some view our sable race with scornful eye,
"Their color is a diabolic dye."
Remember, Christians, Negroes, black as Cain,
May be refined, and join the angelic train.

—Phillis Wheatley, "On Being Brought from Africa to America"

The mother bending over a baby named Shug
chuckles, "Gimme some sugar," just to preface
a flurry of kisses sweet as sugar cane.
Later, when she stirs a spoonful of Domino
into her coffee, who's to tell the story
how a ten-foot-tall reed from the Old World,
on being brought to the New, was raised and cropped
so cooks could sweeten whatever tasted bitter?
Or how grade-A granulated began as a thick
black syrup boiled for hours in an iron vat
until it was refined to pure, white crystal.
When I was a child whose payoff for obeying
orders was red-and-white-striped candy canes,
I knew that sugar was love.
The first time someone called me "sweetheart,"
I knew sugar was love.
And when I tasted my slice of the wedding cake,
iced white and washed down with sweet champagne,
don't you know sugar was love.
One day Evelina who worked for us
showed up with her son Bubba and laughed,
"Now y'all can play together." He had a sweet
nature, but even so we raised a little Cain,
and Daddy told her not to bring him back.
He thought I'd begun to sound like colored people.
She smiled, dropped her eyes, kept working.
And kept putting on weight. She later died of stroke.
Daddy developed diabetes by age fifty-five,
insulin burned what his blood couldn't handle.
Chronic depressions I have, a nutritionist
gently termed "the sugar blues," but damned
if any lyrics come out of them, baby.

Black-and-white negatives from a picture
history of the sugar trade develop
in my dreams, a dozen able-bodied slaves
hacking forward through a field of cane.
Sweat trickles down from forehead into eye
as they sheave up stalks and cart them to the mill
where grinding iron rollers will express a thin
sucrose solution that, when not refined,
goes from blackstrap molasses on into rum,
a demon conveniently negotiable for slaves.
The master under the impression he owned
these useful properties naturally never thought
of offering them a piece of the wedding cake,
the big white house that bubbling brown sugar built
and paid for, unnaturally processed by Domino.
Phillis Wheatley said the sweet Christ was brought
here from Asia Minor to redeem an African child
and maybe her master's soul as well. She wrote
as she lived, a model of refinement, yes,
but black as Abel racing through the canebrake,
demon bloodhounds baying in pursuit,
until at last his brother caught him,
expressed his rage, and rode back home to dinner.
Tell it to Fats Domino, to those who live
on Sugar Hill, tell it to unsuspecting Shug
as soon as she is old enough to hear it.
One day Evelina's son waved goodbye
and climbed on board a northbound train,
black angels guiding him invisibly.
In class he quoted a sentence from Jean Toomer:
"Time and space have no meaning in a canefield."
My father died last fall at eighty-one.
Love's bitter, child, as often as it's sweet.
Mm-mm, I sure do have the blues today:
Baby, will you give me some sugar?

The Cloak of Invisibility

Resisting it at first, I wondered why
Luck had elected to single me out
When subjects more deserving went about
Their business in full visibility.

I favored learning, though, and inch by inch
Sank into knowledge like a nodding sleeper
As the windfall of velvet license deepened.
Not even close-ups made the others flinch—

They shrugged off tingles of warm breath on cheek
Or hand as will-o-the-wisps the dark attracts
And made me privy to whatever facts
Devolve on those whose methods are oblique.

Contagion of invisibility!
Objects caught in the mirror's silver grip,
If I so much as touched them, gave it the slip,
Swept into interstellar darkness, free—

Brocaded screen or acned face, lone mountain
Cabin, oil slick, paperbound Spinoza,
All took shelter under the cloak's *sub rosa*
And drowned appearance in a plunging fountain.

And yet. When the young doctor with downcast eyes
Indicates the gash's stagnant green,
And records a diagnosis of gangrene,
What can't be scraped away, he'll cauterize:

Likewise with me. The morning dawned I saw
Erasure would, eventually, betray
The sunlit chronicle we find our way
By, the Book of Life, that teaches awe

And heals the blind. . . . It seems an endless age
Since I began that volume's restoration,
Coaxing things back to their first destination,
The daily albinism of the page.

Wonderbread

Loaf after loaf, in several sizes,
and never does it not look fresh,
as though its insides weren't moist
or warm crust not the kind that spices
a room with the plump aroma of toast.

Found on the table; among shadows
next to the kitchen phone; dispatched
FedEx (without return address, though).
Someone, possibly more than one
person, loves me. Well then, who?

Amazing that bread should be so weightless,
down-light when handled, as a me
dying to taste it takes a slice.
Which lasts just long enough to reach
my mouth, but then, at the first bite,

Nothing! Nothing but air, thin air. . . .
Oh. One more loaf of wonderbread,
only a pun for bread, seductive
visually, but you could starve.
Get rid of it, throw it in the river—

Beyond which, grain fields. Future food for the just
and the unjust, those who love, and do not love.

Musical Sacrifice

1.

Eisenach, birthplace (in 1685) of J. S. Bach. Close by, on a high hill, Schloss Wartburg, the Thuringian landgraves' ancestral stronghold. Which also sheltered music, judging from Elisabeth's aria in Act II of *Tannhäuser*, a paean addressed to the castle's Great Hall as she waits for the Minnesänger to file in and join her. Music to fortify a fugitive Luther as well, who spent the winter of 1522 there, translating the Bible into dynamic German—and composing hymns. His chorale *Ein' Feste Burg* is most itself when set with strong supporting columns of vertical harmony, like a stone fortress built on some cloudflown crag overseeing the Kingdom. That high hill would also have cast its shadow over the boy Johann shortly after his father's death, which left him an orphan in the care of an exacting older brother.

(*Chorale*)

Passing through streets both small and broad
To Latin school, he hummed the theme
"A Mighty Fortress Is Our God,"
And stared up toward the snowbound castle.

Mother had died, and, after, Father.
Since Adam's fall we all must die,
Yet death stands warrant of our hope
To reach God's glorious court on high.

2.

Prague, baroque outpost of Austro-Hungary, birthplace (in 1883) of Franz Kafka. Praha, the "little mother with sharp claws," whose precincts were topped by a castle—Hapsburg decrees trickling down from it, with consequences for lives being led below in Czech, German, or Yiddish, a populace teeming across cobbled squares, men buttoned into the correct black suit with cravat, a bowler perched on their heads. From Malá Strana to Powder Tower to the Altneu *Shul*, magnetic fields fan out, the stone machine of category and rank in dependable operation.

(*Sprechstimme*)

Choose an unlikely figure, *Kaffeehausliterat*,
minor functionary, Jew, a glass ceiling
overhead, latest subject in the social laboratory,
which has him threading, like a white rat, baroque
labyrinths of alleys, streets, bridges and stairs
that might or might not lead to air and sunlight,

brilliant prospects over the town, intimacy with,
at decent distance, a Father in his stronghold.
But how to enter? *Das Schloss*: "castle" or "lock,"
His key, nothing more than lunch-hour daydreams. . . .
Two fiancées in succession, intelligent,
sensitive; but not right, not right for him.

From the overlords, genteel racial disdain
but partly concealed. Parents, sisters, whose mere
health was a reproach to his own alienated body.
And writing: serious mistake, indeed, transgression, and yet
mandatory. Friends consoled themselves with music: him, though,
it overpowered, "like the sea," or a wall around his mind.

"I am chained to invisible literature with invisible chains."

3. Having journeyed on Foot to Lübeck to Hear Buxtehude, J.S.B. Goes to the Sea and Watches a Horse and Rider on the Sands

(*Toccata*)

Crystalline cold, the rocking thunder
Adjunct to sun in galloping triples,
Sand underfoot, a sea to the right,
High waves of brine collecting to fall
In tumbling explosions, coldest of fires.
Will no wave rise without lifting the sun in replica?
O burn, O freeze, O burn!
Frozen starlike in the salt of a gallop,
A rocking thunder over the dunes, head bent
Forward next to the mane as a freezing stream
Of diamond wind flames across horse and rider,
Sunburned by cold in a rocking sequence
Thundered back by the crash of a wave
Tipping over in a blue-and-gold gallop,
And must it stop playing its well-tuned welter
Of tangled blue manes, its foam-whitened gold?
O freeze, O burn, O freeze!
Rivered burning in the riptide gold,
Salty evangel declaiming triple thunder
That pounds an anvil of sand, the icy keyboard
Headlong hooves thunder over under the blue.
O burn, O freeze, O burn!
From triune Godhead comes the informing Spirit,
And gives us savor of eternity:
The soul borne upward on a faithful mount
By grace alone will scale high Heaven's ramparts.

4. F.K. at Lugano (1911)

(*Waltz*)

Where lemon flowers constellate among dark leaves
and sweeten rising updrafts, water colors the view
for grand hotels, the lake staining deeper blue

at twilight to the flat clank of a church bell.
On the esplanade, yesteryear's white-haired string ensemble
dodders through something *echt* Viennese for guests

in boiled shirtfronts or mauve silk, sipping *aperitivi*:
the allure of lowered eyes, her enigmatic smile
borrowed from Mona Lisa, the late season's fatal

Madame X holding in thrall consumptive poet
or firebrand *metteur en scène*, who in her vibrancies
hears soaring Venusbergs or the final Liebestod.

"My dear Felice," F.K. would write a long year later,
"I feel as though I stood outside a locked door
behind which you live, and which never shall be opened."

Still later, after Franz Ferdinand had been shot
and the Great War unleashed, his daydream antidote
was sifting the potpourri of that lost era, when

malaise had infused the psyche only, a fragrant dust
in Europe's neurasthenic *Götterdämmerung*,
the switch thrown on ranks of Edison lightbulbs,

whose moonglow set the stage for a drugged, experimental
waltz with dark specters, ultimate masked ball
of civilization on the eve of a blood cure.

5. 1722: Anna Magdalena's Little Clavier Book

(*Allemande*)

Among the lessons taught to all below
Are some that bear rehearsal more than once:
"We die, but when death comes we do not know."

My dear Maria died, almost as though
Early departure meant blest deliverance
From painful lessons taught to all below.

Thought of our children constrained to grow
Up orphans, paupers sunk in ignorance,
Could scarcely bear rehearsal more than once.

My early trials, how many years ago,
Were fruit of Father's undue confidence:
We die, but when death comes we do not know.

A second wife, then, fair, but not mere show,
Who'd let no child of Bach's turn out a dunce,
Teaching them lessons all must learn below.

Pride had demanded that I should forego
Love's gentle leadings. Gratefullest penance
Be mine to rehearse, then, and more than once.

Anna requested help with clavier, so
I put together a little book (a dance
Suite), and those ornaments she did not know

The fingering of, at last, began to flow.
Etudes, yet wrought and brought to utterance
By hard or tender lessons learned below—
Some of which bear rehearsal more than once:
We die, but when death comes we do not know.

6.

I discovered them both in 1963 and felt even then something resonant in the juxtaposition, two temperaments completely new and yet somehow familiar. Long, late hours spent replaying the First Brandenburg's Adagio, which conveyed better than any music known to me before what might be called the *mysterium tremendum*, an aura of sacred fear like a pearl-gray cloud between us and unfathomable deity. Oboe, violin, and basses one after the other state and restate the gradually descending theme against a shifting ground of sustained string chords, bass line often the seventh of dominant and secondary-dominant chords. The effect is of hard-pressed determination, the soul testing its powers of understanding when confronted with Creation from the first night until this, the Dorian mode's rugged heft mustered to convey a sense of ineluctable will accomplishing its ends in a world of mute suffering, the human particular left in the dark as to what upheavals might mean or not mean while being subsumed under the Mystery. . . . And yet promised by abrupt modulations into major during the movement's final bars, to keep alive a sense of expectancy and replenishment. Which the last movement delivers.

As for reading Kafka, there will never again be a first encounter like that one, beginning, one cold February night, with *The Trial*, whose blinding glare didn't let me sleep until I'd raced, stumbling and falling, to the end. Transparent style and direct reporting of a character's dilemma activated fiction's deepest resource: identification, the I.D. in this case a set of papers that, far from constituting Josef K.'s protection under the law, in advance condemned him (like all outsiders—racial, cultural, sexual) to a final exclusion. "In the Penal Colony" came next, a courteous peep into Hell, describing some imaginary Devil's Island equipped with a machine designed to engrave sentences like HONOR THY SUPERIORS and BE JUST on the bodies of the condemned and self-condemned. And then The Castle, comedy at its most appalling, a pilgrimage, as much workaday as spiritual, through the frozen corridors of bureaucracy, in which red tape comes to resemble ribbons of blood flowing from the spot where administrative slapstick has struck a bit too hard on the petitioner's head, a stupid grin on his face as the Castle once more denies his re- quest for an audience.

7. 1913: F.K. Publishes His First Book

(*Scherzo in B-minor*)

What, merely because your bumptious friend Brod
insisted you visit busy little Leipzig,
then flung you at *Meineherren* Rowohlt and Wolff;
and merely because those worthies professed to admire
some bleak-spirited trivia you call Meditations,

you bowed and let them serve the public *Kafka*?
Brilliant! Wasn't that you reading Heine last June
at your window, a bluebottle fly buzzing and bumbling
around your ears? Fly lit on page, then *bang!*
you snapped shut your book, which then fell open again:

Black goggle eyes and glassy winglets lay flat
around a speck of dark-red blood, in an instant
kaput and dry. Which triggered your brooding, "I am
that fly, who've done myself in." Ah, now the blunder's
been entombed in hard covers, are you content?

Write, if you must, but banish all thoughts of publishing!

8. 1723: *Johannes-passion* in Leipzig

(*Recitative*)

And it came to pass in those days
that the elders of the Council of Leipzig
summoned candidates for the post of Cantor
for St. Thomaskirche in the city,
among them, Johann Sebastian Bach.
The Council did not rule in his favor
but instead invited Telemann, who declined,
and then Graupner, who also declined.
"As the best could not be obtained,
we must take the second-rate."

So concluded the deliberations.

Yet the Council even so demanded
an example of sacred music wherewith
to judge the celebrated organ master;
thus did he compose a Passion
after the gospel that bore his name.
Not yet satisfied, the elders demanded
a letter of dismissal from the Prince,
his previous employer, and having at last
received it, installed the new Cantor
in June of that year of our Lord.

(*Arioso*)

And are they named St. Thomas Church to doubt
The man He is and works He has done, too?
Almighty God forgive the proud, who flout
Thy commandments, for they know not what they do.

And, Father, grant the strength to keep that head
Unbowed when henchmen come with jeers and flail:
A crown of thorns is well, so He be fed
On that high Love which cannot ever fail.

9. 1917: The Onset

(*Nocturne*)

He had done as much as *will* can perform.
Had even moved into a fine apartment
in the Schönborn Palace, where you might live
decently with a new wife among vases of flowers—
as though you had left Prague behind, were less
in the grip of its musty stone fist.
Yet after her summer visit, he couldn't say.
Who stood, who watched, as her train withdrew, a phrase ringing
in his ears: *The alarm trumpets of nothingness*?

Utter oblivion. Early August doldrums sat
deathlike, burning leaves on all the lindens. . . . One day
he spat fresh blood: his lungs' broken vessels had learned to speak.

To lie awake all night, headboard acreak in the heat,
unfinished drafts invisible in the darkness—
though he could, if need be, feel his way and find them.
A thunderstorm launched its bolts at the sleeping city,
quick volleys of unmeaning light, then giant drumrolls,
alarm trumpets of nothingness. . . . With dawn came rain,
gray light sifting through gently stirred curtain lace.

10.

Musikalisches Opfer, with no article, the noun always translated "Offering," though the German more often means "sacrifice," in the sense of sacred ritual. "Musical Sacrifice," then, one exacted by that musical monarch, Frederick II of Prussia, who had appointed Carl Philipp Emanuel Bach his accompanist in 1740. The elder Bach was several times summoned to the Stadtschloss in Potsdam by his royal admirer, always refusing, until excuses courted insolence. So at last in May 1747, he came to his son's house in Potsdam, half blind, weary, dusty from the journey.

Word of his arrival reached Frederick at Sans Souci, who sent for him immediately, not even giving him time to change into court dress. The king canceled his customary Sunday evening musicale, and "der alte Bach" was ushered into the royal presence. Everyone has heard the story of Frederick's request: Will you sit at the clavier and improvise a fugue for us? The composer asked the king to give him a theme and got a chromatic one in C-minor. Bach clasped his wrinkled hands, then took up the gauntlet to produce a three-part ricercare (the older term for a work with fugal texture), apparently delighting his audience. Then Frederick asked him to improvise a fugue with six voices, which Bach politely said he could not do: even mastery has its limits. On returning to Leipzig, however, Bach wrote out from memory the ricercare in three voices, devised another in six voices (responding to the king's challenge) and spun out as well ten more ingenious canons taking various approaches to the theme. One of these, subtitled "Per tonos," modulates up a whole step in pitch each time the canon repeats, rising higher and still higher, as if scaling a mountain. Not often are technical stunts as expressive as this one, and yet it is less ingenious than other sections of the work, which take canonic texture to even higher levels of complexity. Considering the occasion and the labor voluntarily expended, it's clear why Bach might have given the name he did to the work, printed the following autumn with a dedication to Frederick and sent on to Potsdam like a bread-and-butter note.

Musical Sacrifice, like the more highly developed (though never completed) *Art of the Fugue*, is scored for no instruments in particular, a purely theoretical or pedagogical work reminding us that for Bach creation was happily married to instruction. He sought in these various realizations to produce not only a work of art but an exemplum as well of one or more technical features. No peak of formal difficulty was considered too steep to conquer—as long as sight and breath remained.

11. A Sacrifice for Sans Souci

(*Canon*)

Each year I take a step up the long stairs,
Remembrance flies to youth as to a glade:
The agile keyboard virtuoso tears
Through a fugue no middling fumbler could have played.

Remembrance flies to youth as to a glade
Where will delights in lively conversation
Through a fugue. No middling fumbler could have played
Like that, high ardor at one with calculation.

Where will delights in lively conversation
Take a young man? To marriage, for a start.
Like that high ardor at one with calculation
We have called "music," courtship won her heart.

Take a young man to marriage. For a start,
A child, then two, then more, like steps and stairs.
We have called music "courtship," one her heart
Quickened to hear, at times, quite unawares.

A child, then two, then more, like steps and stairs.
All talented! Whatever music they
Quickened to hear—at times, quite unawares—
I played and taught each one of them to play.

All talented! Whatever music they
May later master, this first shall not rust.
I played and taught each one of them to play
Exactly. Other things the best, l trust,

May later master. This first shall not rust.
Is not fine art, before all else, technique?
Exactly. Other things—the best, l trust—
The soul open to God will surely speak.

Fine art is not, beyond all else, technique.
The agile keyboard virtuoso tears
The soul open to God, who will surely speak
In each resounding step of the long stairs.

12.

Early in *The Castle*, K. attempts to get through to the palace officials by telephone, only to hear a sort of buzzing, "yet not a hum, the echo of voices singing at an infinite distance—blended by sheer impossibility into one high but resonant sound, which vibrated on the ear as if it were trying to penetrate beyond mere hearing." What happens when you associate those high voices with the chorus of Bach's masterworks? Revived by Mendelssohn early in the nineteenth century, the Passions according to Matthew and John eventually became part of standard choral repertory throughout Germany. Wagner knew these consummately theatrical works; nothing easier than for him to consider the anti-Jewish verses of the Passion text in the Gospel of

John as adjuncts (along with Luther's anti-Jewish writings) to his own polemic on behalf of unalloyed Germanic genius. Bach's intentions notwithstanding, when audiences heard the call for crucifixion attributed not to "the people," but to "the Jews," a conscious or unconscious connection was established. Supreme art fueling the onrush of historical evil.

F.K.'s escape from the Shoah was accidental: incurable tuberculosis killed him a decade before Hitler's Reich. TB was also the metamorphosis that had been an excuse for breaking his second engagement to Felice. With no wife to care for him, he had to rely on the efforts of his youngest sister Ottla, who took him to her house in the country and tried to nurse him back to health. He regained enough strength to travel to Berlin, where at last he met Dora Diamant, the companion he had been seeking. A brief period of happiness followed, his first and last. In April of 1923 his friend Hugo Bergmann urged him to make literal the Passover promise of final return, a celebration "next year in Jerusalem." He had been studying Hebrew in an effort to recover the Judaic traditions that secular modernism had replaced. Emigration remained a possibility; but that next year, in terrible pain from tubercular throat lesions, he died, leaving *The Castle* incomplete.

Ottla had married a Czech gentile, a legal status that, after Bohemia had been annexed by Germany, provided her with an immunity from deportation. She refused to profit by the loophole, however; fearing that her children would be implicated, she divorced her husband and registered as a Jew. She was first sent to Terezín and then volunteered to accompany a consignment of orphans being shipped to, she believed, Denmark, but in fact to Auschwitz. There, in October 1943, among searchlights, electric fences, and early snow, she died.

13. *Die Verwandlung*

(*Symphonic poem*)

We are nihilistic thoughts, *kafkas*, jackdaws,
crows in the mind of God,
who, as we do, has bad days—and thought of us

on one of His. Crows hoping to be translated
to Heaven as though unaware Heaven
to be itself requires the absence of crows.
Not to violate those precincts—do you follow, Ottla?—
we must prevent Heaven from thinking of us again.

One afternoon, high up on the Laurenziberg,
our Prague far down below, buildings built
all of smoke, block upon gray block of smoke,
I watched a flock of crows
mount up into the sky in a long line and thought,
Those wings are book bindings, and our books, the steps
of a staircase that breaks off in the sky—
No, rather, a book is a key to the hidden rooms
within the fortress of one's own self,
a black key having the shape of a crow.

I ought to be able to invent words
capable of blowing the odor of corpses in a direction
other than straight into mine and the reader's face.
It was wrong, Ottla, to have allowed those thoughts
to enter your mind—and to bring my illness
to your house, where without the ghost of a complaint
you tried to restore an ailing elder brother
to health again, whether or not he believed you could.
If I could have written myself well again for you!

Once, after you had fed us a small supper,
we sat by the hearth at a low fire,
an orange glow wavering among communicating coals.
A sheaf of gold chrysanthemums sat on top of the piano.
The vase replaced one my elbow had knocked over,
inadvertently, a few days before.
I watched you shovel ashes into a bin, and a daydream,
no, some cinematic phantasm overtook me.
A spark from the coals leapt to my mouth and burned
my lips—but burned away as well the pain of burning.

I saw ashes falling from a great height through space,
falling, falling, as though they might never
get to the bottom of things.
And was tempted to look for their source,
some altar or furnace high up that had produced them;
say, vast numbers of crows heaped up together and burned.
What made me turn away from those images?
Who knows, but they were replaced in thought by a music—
frightening, yet one that I, who always avoided music,
didn't choose not to hear. The figure running across
the keyboard was myself, my footfalls
sounding the notes; and others were running,
fleeing from the catastrophe, each foot
landing on a key as, unawares, we all cooperated.
Was it a fugue of death, a human counterpoint
made by fugitives? Composing not the music
we'd have otherwise produced, but what our flight
from death wrung out of us collectively.

A great hand like the shadow of a bird
approached and began removing, in midflight,
each running figure,
so that voices of the fugue, one by one, dropped out.
Until, at length, no more than two of us remained,
who then stopped running. Oh, but
it was you, Ottla, you were the other,
standing there on a white key, and I, on a black one.
Having so much to say meant we could say nothing,
and nothing inhabited the space between us,
a nothing that bloomed full and golden.
Then I felt myself being taken up; yet didn't tear
my gaze from yours until its silent music
had been translated into darkness,
all my nothing consenting to be absent from the world.
The Holy of Holies opened and nothing was in it.
You were free, Ottla, your name no longer "Kafka,"
and thus were allowed to live. This is why I fell silent—
do you recall?—that dark afternoon by the fire.

14. 1750: J.S.B. Dictates His Last Work From the Deathbed

(*Chorale Prelude*)

When we in greatest need do call
Upon His name, may Jesu send
His strong assistance lest we fall,
And help us make a holy end.

When I in sorest need, in blindness, must
Prepare to bid farewell, my labors done,
The hand that rests upon my brow, I trust
As Love that nothing shall divide me from.

This life has been a prelude and a vale
Where all things teach Thy children Who Thou art.
So may the faithful not forget to hail
Thy cross and glory, Lord, when they depart.

Before Thy throne I shall have trod,
To hear the judgment held in store,
The plea I offer nothing more
Than that Thou diedst for me, O God.

The grace that was and is sufficient guides
Even the lost sheep safely to the fold.
Sing, blessed choirs of angels as of old:
"Nor Sin nor Death prevails where Love abides!"

Amen, Alleluia, Alleluia, Amen, Amen.

A Marriage in the Nineties

They've said the art of poetry resembles,
on one hand, song, with poet as the rara
avis that makes his birdcage play in tune;
it's also been compared to hard labor.

Scrubbing our kitchen tiles today, on all
fours, and humming something like the blues,
I thought of Yeats's line from "Adam's Curse,"
Better go down upon your marrow-bones,

and so forth. How much did a man with servants
know about it? As the decals say,
"I'd rather be writing." But Manhattanites
like us don't keep a car, so where to stick it?

Don't answer that. (Polish, polish, polish.)
It's not that you don't do your share, Chris;
you're a good "husband," women's lib won't help.
Wages of poetry got us at least this far:

we've all of three small rooms to keep in shape.
Just maybe two of these sixth-floor apartments
are decent-sized, and only one tenant straight—
a youngish, ash-blond broker from Belgium,

who that first spring after arriving took
the measure of his present situation
and planted redwood terrace-garden boxes
with pansies by the hundreds, nothing but pansies!

I watched him crouch over small purple-and-yellow
Pekingese faces and waved when he looked up.
Life in the Village. He and a series of girlfriends
haven't seemed flustered at all, they've been nice neighbors.

A marriage in the Nineties. New York City,
if we sign papers, will consider us
"domestic partners." Somehow, though, it feels
more romantic not to. Getting older

pushes mavericks always further toward
the middle class, so why speed up the process?
Insurance offers safety but soaks up feeling—
which brings in risk. Remember Portugal,

the anger we routinely felt for whatever
addict or refugee it was that nicked
our luggage from the car? Those Avis decals
tipped them off, most likely. Property

is theft, granted, but theft of property
also felt like theft. My diary gone,
snapshots we'd taken, worthless to *them*, as well
as other items of "sentimental value."

Both sets of house keys, too, which meant having
a locksmith break into our own apartment
(Russian, moonlighting, his real profession
reproducing Baroque violins).

He scratched his beard and squinted like a watch
repairman at locks he then hauled off and smashed.
At least we got a smile and compassionate handshake,
plus new keys and a bill for two hundred bucks.

Disaster? No, nothing like what happened
to Christophe (our Belgian) the same starcrossed,
snowbound day we returned, his bedroom flooded
by a heating pipe that froze, then cracked, then spewed.

Or to our next-door neighbor Steve, just out
of intensive care for a bout with pneumocystis
during his vacation in Key West,
two balmy weeks with an I.V. in his arm. . . .

We're very lucky. No microbes have broken
in and made off with our lives or health.
Nor are we homeless like Devane, the guy
who sits all day outside our building, hailing

strangers or neighbors like us who halfway know him.
Time and again I've said, "Devane, a man
as smart as you has no business on the street."
He agrees, yeah-yeah, and blames cocaine and booze

which he plans to kick someday. Today?
Well, no, it helps him stand the cold and damp,
but one great morning. . . ! He also tells me he's
bisexual, but that one I let pass.

As a schoolboy in, say, Brussels, Christophe—
funny, it just occurs to me that you
and he have the same name—may well have read
Pascal's *Pensées*, as I did back in college.

He'd probably recognize the one that says,
"The more intelligence one has the more
people one finds original. Commonplace
people see no difference between men."

Devane, for instance, calculating each
potential donor's quirks and soft spots so
he can "articulate sweet sounds together,"
magic words to make it rain down gold

or silver, any tribute but the pennies
he loathes but must of course pretend to want.
Or Steve next door, who says he prayed to survive
once more because he hadn't yet determined

his true identity and what he's here for.
Or us, sweetheart, this February 14th,
which I didn't think of in time to find
a present. Middle age's curse, defective

memory—as good an excuse as any
"for getting it all down." That, and a chance
to image feeling with exactitude,
love for an irreplaceable hunk, whatever.

From Lisbon to Beijing to Brussels, song
breaks forth to say inclinations have changed:
"The life devoid of sentiment is not
worth living," a news flash ricocheted off Telstar,

dense wavelength webwork of the global village
where we make a present of ourselves
to stranger and neighbor, hoping it's the thought
that counts. Come this June, I'll write mine out

and see if Christophe wants to anthologize
one more *pensée* with those in his terrace boxes.
To you, Chris, hearts and flowers of the day,
and kitchen tiles that will just have to do.

Parallels

A song of praise runs parallel to fact.
What psalms present is pure experience.

As mirrors praise or blame the facts they show,
So facing mirrors judge themselves alone:

Each in mirroring mirroring in each,
Reflects contrary counterfeits of truth,

A glass-green emptiness in shrinking frames.
Contempt? It's nothing but reversed self-loathing.

Imagine, instead, an act of conciliation,
Someone recalling how much there was to praise.

Imagine a plain with tracks to the far horizon,
A pair of rails intent on the same point.

Parallel lives. . . . Since everything that rises
Must converge, perhaps they're moving upward?

CONTRADICTIONS
(2002)

Whether

Whether anger quickens a lagging stride,
and periodic burn-offs in the forest
revitalize exhausted soil and flora—.
Whether we should take pleasure in the wildcat

jubilation of a lightning bolt
that whips its silver vein of genesis
through the night sky, flash-photo of a white
birch upended, the root-system buckled

to swollen thunderheads—. And whether naming
an offense amounts to sour grapes and common
bitterness, or even the conceited nonsense
of unwashed yahoo multitudes, a yawping

insult to civilized behavior—. Whether
a July rainstorm, even when it drenches
the unprepared pedestrian and befuddles
traffic, might be extravagant, a joy,

like the whoops and escalating bop glissandos
of Gillespie's upraised horn, cascading pitches
a countersong to meteoric chalk marks
Perseids burn across the House of Leo—.

And whether peaceful ecstasy might float
up from a fifteen-second avalanche
reflected in the skier's goggles, his jacket
a spark of scarlet on the topmost slope,

waiting for the homeward track to clear.

The Mousetrap

for Nikolas Stangos and David Plante

'Tis the day after Christmas, London, Boxing Day, twelve noon,
A.D. 2000. Outdoors,
as *Hamlet's* sentry (Act I, Scene i) says, "Not a mouse stirring."

On Baker Street, though, once you stir, you'll spy, through parted curtains,
a matron dressed in blue,
boxing up surplus presents to be sent on to the needy.

(Thoughtful friends proposed and underwrote my holiday,
three weeks in Marylebone. . . .
So, church mouse, rack your brains, and find a way of conveying thanks.)

No special rep for largesse stars the name of Arthur C. Doyle,
whose alter ego lodged
here at 221b, now "The Sherlock Holmes Museum."

Trinkets in its shop window dangle from a dozen hooks.
And the cleaner's farther down
sports this notice, save the mark, in gold: WE WILL DYE FOR YOU.

Today's also the Feast of Stephen. They wrapped *him* up, all right,
with punches to the gut,
left jabs of stone, and, match done, sepulcher carved out of same.

(A boxed red set of martyrdom the *Golden Legend* gave
the poor—stonemasons, some
of them, and bricklayers, whose patron pious black humor named him.)

Underground's the quickest transport to my matinée,
Agatha Christie's *Tourist*
Trap, I mean, *The Mousetrap*, Guinness record for long runs.

St. Martin's Theater is crammed, cramped, dowdy; in its creaky
way, stately, with
the columns and dark panels of a country house in Kent.

Curtain up on blackness: screams, a scuffle. Follows a none
too bright comedy
of murders enlivening a B&B named Monkswell Manor.

Christie's gambits resemble that old board game *Clue*: "Colonel Mustard
did it; in the Den;
with the Knife," we'd guess and keep on guessing till we solved the case.

The play's canonic theme song, "Three Blind Mice," has its own perp,
an unnamed farmer's wife,
who cut off their tails, et cetera, before they "bought the farm."

Don't try to grasp a Mother Goose rhyme, and even less our pomo
poetry or Ophelia's
word-salads, which consumers "botch up fit to their own thoughts."

The Prince of Denmark's play within the play's the same sly thing,
a detective Rorschach set
to catch the conscience of the king... and titled *The Mouse-trap*.

Coincidence. The minute it strikes, take cover, private eye!
Christie's got designs
on you. If conscience is the game, though, how does she figure it?

As a purblind mouse, I guess, whose twitching nose sniffs something rotten
and ferrets out repressed
mischief—each playgoer, A.C. suggests, a Mickey Rex.

*

Curtain, bows. An actor moments earlier nailed as culprit
steps forward and makes us
flattered accessories pledge not to give away the ending.

(Bait that initiates would dangle, keeping the box office
busy for almost half
a century, the diehard run itself an extra hype.)

Meanwhile, the author's books have sold, worldwide, a *billion* copies.
Why do we so love murder?
A mystery (like the Incarnation) that still remains unsolved.

My guess: "Detective fiction's our response to the withdrawing
tide of faith, when God,
if not Old Nick, was snuffed by evolution, astrophysics.

To prove no gates of Hades yawned, our inner centurion
stalked the Place of the Skull
and whipped out tools. In the lab, with science, clues suggest, *we* done it.

And then felt guilty. . . ." Plausible? Even applaudable.
But, as I step outside
and slog through mist and dark, more dialogue: *So typical.*

Always boxing yourself in with abstract speculation,
poor substitute for feeling
your concrete circumstances. True, but it helps protect me. *From?*

Peanut gallery catcalls like, "Geez, will someone please toss
a dropcloth over his cage."
Emulate princeling spleen re blacklisting, skulduggery?

No thanks. Abstraction springs the lock and helps us build (archaic
smile in place) a verbal
construct—thank you, St. Stevens—lighter, limberer than stone.

*

Home to New York again. The months tick by to strike late March,
today's park ramble ending
at the Cloisters' gate. I'll see a Gothic amulet starred with diamonds;

a pear tree's angular espalier fixed to weathered limestone;
the Unicorn in his paddock.
For only a Virgin could detain him—one like that ingénue

there in Campin's *Annunciation*. The facts: St. Gabriel did it
with a breathing ray of light
in the betrothed's neat inglenook, she reading a book of hours.

Flanked, too, by other clues: a candle just then snuffed; a polished
ewer; a lily Ophelia
never caroled. Fact, symbol, fused in oil paint fluent as chrism.

Left-panel donors, keen first-nighters in rich trappings, queue up.
In the right, St. Joseph's shop,
where he sits drilling, planing, nailing, top-hinged wooden shutters

hooked open inward to admit a Flemish view of Nazareth. Bend
closer. On the sill,
contraption for sale: a mousetrap, cocked for action. Ah. He'd read

Augustine: "The Cross of the Anointed was the Demon's mousetrap."
Build the best prototype,
and the world will beat a path to your door. Then clemency pleas can be

lodged with the carpenter's wife, I guess? From felicity abstracted,
the saeculum's long run
designed—alas, poor Yorick—to make a case for each wounded name.

Jerusalem

Then keep thy heart. . . .

—Melville, *Clarel*

They will lift up their heads:
the Lion Gate, St. Stephen's, the New,
Jaffa, and, last, the Gate of Dung.
The gates will lift up their heads
that the King of Glory may come in.

As Judah means "Praised," its chief city will be
more highly praised, the ramparts and towers
of David's citadel praised and exalted.

*

Come this far, how close the door on what
not even they had stubbornness enough to bar?
The Rock where Isaac, his wrists bound tight,
saw above him a face clench in agony
moments before an angel dove down to stay
Abraham's hand is now perpetual,
preserved in the furnace of tradition
along with that ram whose horn became the shofar.

—Or is it rock as fact, one of the sights,
coated with dust and roofed with a golden dome
reverberant with a murmured sura
expanding on the Prophet's airborne nocturnal
journey, which fixed him like a star
on the cusp of the crescent moon?

*

Just as the present-day pilgrim goes from station
to station in a loud array of discount tours,
tenants have reconstrued the basilica
of the Holy Sepulcher as real estate
for hereditary zeal to balkanize

among several sects. Each has its sharply
defended square yardage of theology, but none

equals that stone niche off to one side where an oil lamp's
starred wick baffles the sway of archaic shadows.

*

The Temple abides in its myth
but also in limestone fact, at least the part
Roman demolition experts failed
to pound into undatable rubble.
Foundation Wall, you won't be alone again,
alive with the Shekhinah's quiet thunder,
bloodwarm dovecote of fissured building blocks
into which ten thousand handwritten
praises or lamentations have flown.

*

And Via Dolorosa toils south from Gabbatha's
courtyard, where a few detached centurions
gave their charge the prescribed flogging
before sending him on his forced march.
A path useless to retrace without spiriting away
two millennia or any obstacle
to contemplation of punished flesh at ground zero
staggering forward under a massive wooden T,
palm fronds still underfoot, but dry and broken,
whispering hosannas no one hears.

Because a Procurator exercised available
options, the name "Pilate" survives globally
on the lips of millions when the Credo's recited
tenets descend into history and make it faith.

*

What was truth? What will it be?
For the condemned whose breath comes shorter and shorter,
"Even death may prove unreal at the last"—unreal,

like the sound of a tree fallen to earth
far from any ear, or any human ear.
When the body atoned to its trunk and limbs toppled
out of time, did it finally become audible
to his listeners? To some. To Clarel, and for later
pilgrims who risked as much as one step beyond doubt.

No other dispatch could outdistance the silence
following on that farewell to his friend—
who, standing at the Place of the Skull,
heard him say, "Woman, behold thy son,"
as prelude to, "Behold thy mother."
Seeing where sons of earth were bound to go,
from that day forth he housed a second mother under his roof.

Lift up your heads.

A Walrus Tusk from Alaska

Arp might have done a version in white marble,
the model held aloft, in approximate awe:
this tough cross-section oval of tusk,
dense and cool as fossil cranium—

preliminary bloodshed condonable
if Inupiat hunters on King Island may
follow as their fathers did the bark of a husky,
echoes ricocheted from roughed-up eskers

on the glacier, a resonance salt-cured
and stained deep green by Arctic seas, whose tilting floor
mirrors the mainland's snowcapped amphitheater.
Which of his elders set Mike Saclamana the task

and taught him to decide, in scrimshaw, what was so?
Netted incisions black as an etching
saw a way to scratch in living infinitives
known since the Miocene to have animated

the Bering Strait: one humpback whale, plump,
and bardic; an orca caught on the ascending arc,
salt droplets flung from a flange of soot-black fin. . . .
Farther along the bone conveyor belt a small

ringed seal will never not be swimming, part-time
landlubber, who may feel overshadowed by the donor
walrus ahead. And by his scribal tusk, which stands
in direct correspondence to the draftsman's burin,

skillful enough to score their tapeloop ostinato,
no harp sonata, but, instead, the humpback whale's
yearning bassoon (still audible if you cup
the keepsake to your ear and let it sound the depths).

And Then I Saw

My body, laid out on a marble slab.
Naked but for a linen sheet tucked under
Its chin, as though to keep the patient warm.

A solemn band approached; identified
The late departed with what looked like mingled
Relief, mild satisfaction, and bereavement.

One of them took away an arm—the right,
Was it?—and loped off with a spring in his step.
Which prompted others to do likewise: here

A shoulder (suitable for crying on),
there a foot, there an eye and there an ear.
Plump already, one scooped out the belly.

Just who you'd imagine claimed the head.
Not the one I hoped tugged loose a rib.
Some, by no means all, I knew as friends;

But felt no bitterness, instead, acceptance.
This, while watching their several withdrawals,
Travelers moving farther out and deeper

Into the ringing distance—who all began
To flourish, somehow more intently themselves
Than they had earlier resolved to be.

Was glad of that, despite a fit of shivers
(Simple human nature still presiding)
When I took note of the rummage that remained,

Wishing a greener plot had been marked out
For what had breathed with so much spark and promise.
My turn, then, to come forward for a closer

Look; and, since no one else had carried off
That steady, flexibly strung pump at rest
Beneath the sternum, take it for my own,

Sensing its mute but anchored trust that parts
Lucky for others would befriend as well—
Oh love—even the heir that flesh once named.

Seeing All the Vermeers

Met Museum, 1965, the first
I'll see, his *Young Woman Sleeping*.
Stage right, bright-threaded carpet flung over the table
where a plate of apples, crumpled napkin
and drained wineglass abut the recapped pitcher.
Propped by one hand, her leaning drowse,
behind which, a door opens on the dream, dim, bare
but for a console and framed mirror—or a painting
too shadowed to make out. Next to it,
(certitude) one window, shuttered for the duration. . . .

That dream also timed *me* out, a lull in the boomeranging
hubbub of the staggering city I'd just moved to.

*

In the Frick's *Officer and Laughing Girl*, spring sunshine
entered left, partly blocked by the noncom suitor's hat-brim,
wide, dark as seduction, conquest. A map dotted with schooners
backed her fresh elations, the glass winking at them both. . . . He'd see
why, in a later day, crewcut recruits were shipping out to Nam;
and she, why the student left was up in arms against the war.

*

In '67, Ann and I spent a graduate year in Paris;
and lived in the Louvre, too, along with *The Lacemaker*—
self-effacing, monumental, an artisan
whose patience matched the painter's, inscribed
in tangling skeins of scarlet oil against an indigo
silk cushion. Silent excruciation
among toy spools framed the bald paradox
termed "women's work," disgracing anything less
than entire devotion to labor entered into. (That May,
a million demonstrators marched up the Champs Elysées.)

*

From there to Amsterdam and *The Little Street*,
where innate civility distilled a local cordial, free
from upheaval, from dearth *and* opulence, each brick

distinct, their collectivity made credible
by a chalky varicosis that riddled foreground façades.
A century's successive mortars filled those cracks,
nor will the figures down on hands and knees in the foreground
stand up again till they've replaced that broken tile.

The *Woman in Blue Reading a Letter* calmed misgivings
with the global trust that swelled her body, a soft counterweight
to expeditions tracked across the weathered map behind.
A newfound Eden, festooned with portents, history
piloting ship and cargo across the wrinkling sea.

The *Maidservant Pouring Milk*'s power to see
in threadbare clothes and plain features a meek radiance
made of *caritas*, doesn't need words... But since I do,
call her a velvet motet developed in blue, in scaled-down
yellow-green that I could hear, the resonant stillness
centered on movement's figment, cream paint paying out
a corded rivulet at the cruse's lip. Crusty loaves, nail-holes
in plaster, and knuckles roughened by scalds and scrubs
witnessed to the daily immolation, performed as first light
tolled matins from a dutch-gold vessel hooked to the wall.

*

By train to Den Haag, to see the *View of Delft's* ink-black
medieval walls and bridge, barges anchored on a satin
water more pensive than the clouded blue above,
where one tall steeple took its accolade of sun.
(Proust's "patch of yellow wall" I couldn't find, though.)

The *Girl in a Turban* looked like Anne Wiazemsky,
Godard's new partner, whom we'd seen in his latest film.
Liquid eyes, half-parted lips, a brushstroke ancillary

to fable highlighting the weighty pearl at her earlobe,
her "Turkish" costume stage-worthy, if she ever chose to act.

*

By then it was set: No matter how many years or flights
it took, I'd see all of Vermeer—which helps explain
the Vienna stop we made that spring, and our instant beeline
to *An Artist in His Studio* (called, today, *The Allegory of Fame*).
What to make of the Artist's bloomers, outmoded even then—

and why would his model hold book and clarion, standing
before the mapped Low Countries? If that anesthetized mask
on the table near her denied the chandelier its candles,
then who hung a tapestried curtain in the left foreground?

Vermeer; but his meaning subverts comment, always
less hypnotic than the surface itself, a luminous
glaze adhering to receding frames in series,
chromatic theaters for featured roles that also kindle
fervor in their supporting actor, the secret soul.

*

Strike me dumb on first seeing *The Astronomer*
in Guy de Rothschild's study—well, a photograph of it
in an '80s coffee-table book, *The Great Houses
of Paris*. Not long after, thanks to philanthropy
and the tax structure, it devolved upon the state.
Semester break that winter, McC. and I jetted to France,
entered the Louvre's new glass pyramid and fought
dense crowds to where he hung, *The Lacemaker's* late consort.
In a brown studio, his fingers reading the globe,
he sat, immovably dutiful to calculations
devised ad hoc to safecrack the star-studded zodiac.

*

I was one of the visitors tiptoeing
through Isabella Gardner's house in Boston

decades before the heist, which to this day
remains unsolved. But balance one instance
of good luck against a trip made to Ireland
in '86, missing by only a few months
the Beit Collection's *Lady Writing a Letter*.
Paid so often now, the compliment of theft
puts a keen edge on our art pilgrimages:
The icon may be gone when you arrive.

That fall, I lived in London's Camden Town,
writing on . . . call them stateside topics; and soon
tubed up to Kenwood House, relieved to find
their prime collectible unstolen—its potential
as ecphrastic plunder not apparent at the time.

(A sonnet, no less, completed earlier in New Haven,
qualified me for that satire on the Connecticut bard
besotted with Vermeer. Still, subjects could be barred
in advance only if they and poems were the same gadget.
Disbelief, you're suspended, even for the standard
gloat over shots knocked back at the Cedar Tavern,
ca. 1950, with Pollock and de Kooning.)

Here then was Kenwood's *Lady with Guitar*, in corkscrew
curls, lemon jacket trimmed with ermine, lounging
like some hippie denizen of Washington Square,
strumming for the nth time his secondhand Dylan. . . .
Maybe they heard her, too, the National Gallery's
paired women portraits, each playing a virginal,
both in silk dresses, one seated, one standing—
Profane and Sacred Love, if the old allegory fits.

A trip from London to Edinburgh produced, beyond
the classic-Gothic limestone city grimed with soot,
an early *Christ in the House of Mary and Martha*,
conceived before the painter's parables began unfolding
at home in Delft. Still, Martha's proffered pannier is as real
as the bread it holds, and Jesus' open hand, rendered
against clean table linen, as strong and solid as Vermeer's.

*

A chill, damp March in Dresden with Chris.
We'd begun with the Berlin State Museum's holdings
and then trained down on our way to Prague.
The Gemäldegalerie, quiet as a church, listened
while beads of tarnished rain pelted the skylights.
Works known from reproductions offered themselves
to the gray ambient, visibly conscious
of having survived Allied firebombs fifty years
earlier and a postwar Ice Age that slammed home,
then froze every bolt in the Eastern sector.
Young Vermeer's *The Procuress* makes love for sale
push beyond the sour analogue
of art-as-commerce into distinct portraits,
comedic types you have and haven't seen before,
caught up in cheerful barter while wine flows
at a balustrade draped with carpet and a fur cape.
The client's left hand could have been mine,

weighing down a pretty shoulder (and the bodice),
but not the right, poised to let fall a coin
into her open palm. Men's hunger for sex
and poverty's for comforts—an old story,
mean or tragic, and never finally resolved.

*

Having missed Her Majesty's *The Music Lesson*, lent
over the years to several exhibitions, guess who danced
when told that it would grace the show to end all shows
scheduled in Washington, the fall of '95.
And other hard-to-sees from Brunswick and Frankfurt—
jubilation—were included also, plus
apprentice works on pagan or religious themes.
Long caterpillar of a line, composed of hundreds
come to worship art and its obsessive love of life.
An hour's wait on aching legs, and in we go:
The Geographer, taking his place by *The Astronomer*;
Ireland's letter-writer, look, recaptured, and now restored

to the public; a *View of Delft*, cleaned so thoroughly
you couldn't miss that patch of yellow—not a wall,
Proust got it wrong, instead, a roof. . . Sheltering involuntary
memories of countless choked-up viewers,
whose gazes added one more laminate of homage
to a surface charged with how many hundred-thousands now.

From the permanent collection—why?—I saw as though
I never had the *Woman Weighing Gold,* some twenty years
(gone, and still here) since that first visit (Walter with me)
to the National Gallery. By word-origin Galilees,
international through their holdings, these cathedrals
of art draw in the faithful that faith in art has summoned
for mutual appraisal, what we are seen in what we see.

Hence the scales at center canvas Vermeer suspended
from her fine-boned hand, the face all understanding
and, so, forgiving all. Nevertheless, the great maternal
judge weighs one gold (a ring? a coin?) against a smaller gold,
in gloom as dark as the Day of Wrath, whose millennial
trumpet tears away a final veil.

So human error
will yield, her calm demeanor says, to *Pax caelestis*
and dawn break forth in perpetual light transforming
breath, strife, treasure, theft, love, and the end of love,
into its own substance—strong, bright beam of Libra rising
step by step up the scale to Eden and a countenance
the soul, made visible, is now accorded grace to see.

Around us, heads bent toward a morning vintaged
more than three hundred years ago. Manifold delight
wearing Nikes, Levi's, parkas; students, grizzled veterans,
young mothers, teachers, painters—awestruck, whispering
Heavens! Just look at that!—his New World public.

Tables
(2013)

Resources

Late May remakes the park, even
the part laid out behind wrought iron
fence railings, one pigeon on promenade,
crisp feathers a not so common
cocoa and dishrag-gray, the compact head
ticking along fast forward,
a shimmering silk rainbow as its collar.
Heavy leafage, pollen and nectar poured
from the locust flowers' galactic cloud. . . .
Breathe in the fragrant troposphere, then pause:
and let today recover its first cause.

*

I've been paging through compendia and sources
to find that timeless tale, the one in which
a peasant princess wearing star-bright pearls
(the dowry offered by a guardian witch)
drops her gaze and lets a sneering rival
snatch away the favor. Who, when she forces
its clasp shut, shrieks to see her pillage shrivel
into a snarl, a torque of snakes and lizards—
the same for all wearers but the fair and gentle.

*

A Fifties living room. "Consider the *source.*"
For emphasis, her last word's octave leap
struck a dulcimer that rang out silver
as wires glinting in permanent elderly
waves, waves a tearful grandson shouldn't muss.

Consolation was built on fortitude.
Dunces spat venom, ragged us with their cheap
jokes, but disgrace was theirs alone, the fruit
of a defective character bedeviled
by our brain's reptilian taproot. "It's misplaced

response to abuse they've endured themselves.
Treat them as *you* should treat them, not as they
do you. Wherever we are known as ourselves,
there's love enough. Say, curly head, who made us?
Then raise your eyes, lamb, and consider the Source."

*

Pre-summer aftershimmer lingers late,
the last knife, plate and cup not put away
till well beyond eleven. What's made me
burn insomnia's glaring kilowatt,

red chips stacked on the actuarial table?
A decade's grace; then sky-high interest on the Debt. . . .
Life-lender, you've let it stay outstanding, yet
collection agencies all know my name.

Lamplight. A cloudburst of bygones. One free
hand sprawled on facing pages of a book.
"Call in thy death's head there; tie up thy fears."
Smithy of resource, the ringing anvil changing
what sleep's lithe silver ouroboros took
from one day's solo round, till the prologue clears:

Late May remakes the park, even
the part laid out behind wrought iron
fence railings, one pigeon on promenade. . . .

Dinner Theater

Characters treading not quite level pine
Boards number, first off, Pitcher, sweating beads
Of coolant on her Delft-blue leaves and birds.
Then enter Sirloin, crusty, rare, supine,

Giving his aromatic agony
Away in pink tears drained into the dark
Platter's symmetrically branching tree.
Sharp Knife starts bantering with Mrs. Fork—

You know, metallic whispers re Parsnip,
The fossil he's been trying to butter up.
Pepper's gambits are pungent, but poor Salt
Gets maudlin as the meal grinds to a halt.

And now the attentive, worn-out Napkins move
Toward lips whose service, too, resembles love.

Window on the World

Time after time a glitch immobilized the screen
At *Windows Is Shutting Down*, the program icon hanging

Fire in paradoxical support of its sign-off
Caption during that long month of graveyard shifts

And pre-dawn vigils I spent sifting online fallout
Of terror, pity, and insight posted to the globe.

Nine-Eleven, Nine-Eleven, hear it, a ravaged
SOS, our call to arms and talisman,

The dateline turning septic with its subtext, spun
Out by the Web's ten thousand arachnes, so many

Forwarding Auden's "Those to whom evil is done
Do evil in return." And done again by enraged

Coevals, sheer reaction's critical mass redoubling
Topical fission, escalation, devolution,

A huge acridity that spikes air-quality graphs,
That floats down on a waterproofed black jacket's yellow

And gray stripes as the bearded fireman doffs his helmet
At the sky, twin tear-streaks guttering a mask of ashes.

**

Time travel: From our early- '70s Grand Street loft space
In pre-consumer-heaven SoHo, W.

And I had watched and clocked the towers' floor by floor
Ascent, a postwar symbol of extra-military

Triumph, material and pop culture scoring where
Napalm, exfoliants and M-16s had failed.

So empire might not seem passé, tired Unity bowed
And underwrote a new production, Concept Two,

The male North Tower boasting its TV broadcast mast,
The female South, an observation deck for tourists.

A few floors down, designer restaurant, entitled
Windows on the World: Where better celebrate

The publication of a poet's debut volume?
One, we liked back then to patronize posh venues;

Two, a comment on its blue and orange jacket
Had called the book "a new window onto the world."

Consolation for not being rated the latest star—
A Seidman, Burkhart, Jordan, Piercy, or Blackburn—

It mostly worked, though befriending envy sometimes hissed,
Those years I spent cooling my heels outside fame's shortlist.

But not that day. From our table on floor 107,
I heard the City launch its anthem, steep windows framing

Brooklyn and Verazzano Bridges, the Woolworth Building,
Five high-rise mirrored boxes, Liberty, and the Harbor.

On top of the world, bask, green bardlet, in those spacious
Skies, don't aim your telephoto lens at the future.

* *

Where you'd see you, weathered, silvered, skipping farewell
Glances at a town three decades your home base.

For fame, whatever else it's not or doesn't do,
At least pays bills, the scrape and cramp that youth can finesse

Costing the veteran pain, angst, and sleeplessness.
Advanced degrees in urbanity packed up, July

2001, I dropped the gear in Drive and launched out
On the road, no landfall planned before late August.

**

Those not tube-addicts will understand how, absent
A shaken call from a friend reporting the first strike,

One nauseated witness fewer would have seen, no,
Felt in his gut both deathbolts and the dual collapse.

Felt through the media—TV, Net, and, before
Blackout, cell phones. Somehow I got through to friends,

None of them missing but all choked by poison gas,
Paralyzed speechless with the inconceivable.

**

Because the dead disown inflated claims, I have to
Question several statements made about the towers:

"An architectural masterpiece." No, they were *tall*, some
High-rises elsewhere taller, and many better designed.

"The hub of U.S. geopolitics and trade."
No, few that worked there qualified as global players.

"Site of the first homeland attack since Independence."
No, see 1812, the Civil War, Pearl Harbor.

"The modern era's worst disaster." No, consider
Stalingrad, Dresden, Hiroshima, the Holocaust.

"New York's chief symbol." Not, in all honesty, to most,
No match for the Bridge, Ellis Island, or Liberty.

**

But place detachment beside a sense of mutilation
Inferno's aftermath would trigger six weeks later

When my night flight on American approached
Ground Zero. Spotlit, twenty-four/seven rubble clearance

Replaced twin peaks naïveté once took for granted
In the downtown spreadsheet printout of Manhattan's skyline.

Pilgrimage to the site required a mask to filter
Fumes that stank of burnt synthetics and calcium.

I choked up gazing at that iconic shard, a giant
Upended metal thumb-piano keyboard whose ragged

Elegy roaring earthmovers snuffed out as they
Processed remains of two thousand and more deceased.

Who won't be back. And yet, almost as though to highlight
Absence, TV movie reruns these past months

Have been reviving, in how many slots, an image
Both stricken and eternal: standard chopper panning

Shots of the postcard skyline thrusting at us, and, lo,
The stereophonic comeback Symbol, tall as life.

**

Mortality, box-cutter in hand, conquers all,
A cockpit-crasher, terminating our dazed pilots,

Jamming the vessel's forward mandate. . . Does that senior
Chef taking bread from ovens in his vintage kitchen

Lofted among the clouds, detect invisible
Omens in the autumn light?—a bass-clef hum,

Endtime launched on its unyielding slalom, twin
Convergence that will call for shutdown once our client,

The kamikaze who refused to book a table,
Shows up to firebomb celebration's ever-afters.

**

Befriending soul, when lethal smoke begins to rush
From the broken towers' crematory, will we hang back

In burning topicality? *No*, sings the window.
Hold hands, eyes meeting as they never have before.

Today your tandem launches out on visionary
Sunlight, to cast its lot with a world without end—

One extra encore for a pair upheld in zero
Gravity, anti-Lucifers, twin morning stars,

United Symbol here that nothing puts asunder,
Love's company unlost so long as love proves life.

COALS

No two alike, exchanging nuances
Of fervor, each core permeable

To wingbeats lit with utterance's
Halation, golden streambed gravel

Immersed in a baptismal shimmer
Nearly inaudible but never stilled....

Great-grandmother's coal fires winters
Back in the scriptural forties filled

Our rooms with thick carbonic reek—
With prophesying infrareds

So fierce they stung (and sting) the cheek
That then put up with and now laments

Old age's kiss. She'd say: *Repay*
Evil with good, our sole defense.

Kindness heaps coals of fire on hatred,
Ill will. . . Then bring one from the grate

For lips more drawn to blame than to amends.

CORN, ALFRED D., JR. 34833361 T44 450

Try and muster the first unshaven dogface
to call them "dog tags," sardonic smile aimed
at a pair of steel and nickel leaves die-stamped
with his name, a license to kill or be killed.

Like some legendary bullet-stopping Bible,
gemini chiming shields suspended
on a beaded chain and slung around
infantrymen's necks must from time to time
have saved their lives. When not, the medics would
at least know where to ship parts left behind.

A ball of string, the globe has spun and shrunk
since Daddy's hitch, the upshot, any conflict
within days goes worldwide. ID'd and daily fed
into databanks, what's my answer when a voice
high in the nonexistent dome overhead
asks how I view our military safeguards?

Good thing those soldiers couldn't see into
the future. Their bead-chain rosaries failed to say
what world was in the pipeline, and previews
wouldn't have much helped steel the resolve
of a man slogging on through muck and ordnance.

A pathetic booster, I have to leave him there
in his determined past, where he can do his bit
for Mother and us, the jingle dangling on his chest
spelling his name (and my name, once removed),
urging him not to let down the brand; also helpful
in case he fell, too messed up to be recognized.

Anthony in the Desert

To be filled with that hallowed emptiness
The hermit sojourns in a desert cave.
Fasting and prayer will make seclusion safe,
His daily bread, each word the Spirit says.

Chimera stirs and rears her dripping head;
A slack-skinned reptile puffs and makes a face;
Vile, harrowing nightmares shimmer through long days;
The sun beats a brass gong and will not set.

Faint shadow on cave walls, you foretell grief
Or joy, not known till whose the profile is:
Love itself may corrupt and then deceive
Its object, hiding venom in a kiss.
Anthony kneels, embraces his fierce lot,
And hears: *Be still, and know that I am God.*

ALF LAYLAH WA LAYLAH

The Book of a Thousand Nights and a Night

Sesame opens on a trove of palm-tree locales
From the Indus to the Maghreb, Baghdad, Mecca,
Damascus, Cairo, a realm where chance and waywardness
Ripple what dunes flank the snakelike silk roads,
Where Allah, may He be praised, patterns Creation,

Sending djinn, tsunamis of coiling sea serpents

Or birds broad as mountains, to punish wrongdoers
And reward the good—whose names come twinned,
Sindbad the Seaman and Sindbad the Landsman,
Or Abu Kir the Dyer and Abu Sir the Barber,
Personae spun like wool on fortune's wheel

Into narratives sprouting ancillary tales

Set in turn with cameo fables, a nested sequence
Of concentric matrices linked by one umbilical,
The hypnotic, purred gestations of Scheherazade,
Plotter of addictive, oil-lamp-lit recitatives
For a thousand nights and one, destinies imaged

So as to convert impending death into audience,

A pragmatism delirious as a carpet theorized
Along the lines of cosmogony's tautly strung
Chaos, yet weaving, too, a human precinct, a mihrab
Where prayer is texted to the Compassionate,
The All-giving, whose hands hold keys to worlds

Seen and unseen, that His mercies may not cease.

Toys in the Hospital Gift Shop

A stubby zebra with wallpaper stripes;
The hacksaw gape of a felt crocodile;
A sleek fire engine and its coiling hose;
Hand-puppet clowns with green or orange hair:

One of these should soothe our kindergarten
Convalescent, who'll let it freely range
The linen snowfield mountained by his knees
Till sleep's slow carrousel-spin times him out. . . .

What do toys want to say, why *are* they us,
Adults still snapping up and treating children
To bits of fluff that make us laugh, a lure
For the sandman's bag of animated films?

Prophets used to call the worldly sphere
A hospital, each wounded soul its patient.
Supposing our evolving globe's a wind-up
Toy, too, designed to charm its ailing Maker,

Who names deific maladies, or heals them?
What tragicomic acts provide distraction,
Teasing away eternal tears and boredom
Till evening starts to roll in, pain subsides,

And humor's snow-plow clears the path to sleep?
Whose muffled advent also snuffs Creation—
Its toys, beforehand, voicing a rote petition:
May we recur as players in your dream.

First Dictionary

Its frontispiece a grizzled Noah Webster
In fresh-tied neck-cloth, gazing calmly westward.

Thirteenth birthday present for a searcher-
Out of meanings, who grasped that reasoned nurture

Had landscaped lexic woodlands to a plain
Instructive playing field where scrubs could train.

Also, it featured small line-drawings, four
Or maybe five per page: the human ear

In cross section; a rhesus monkey rather
Resembling the mild lexicographer

Who'd pegged him as a primate, hence our dumb
Cousin. Cuts for the alphabetic thumb

Index were sills that staggered down to a cave
Or hatch that opened for explorers brave

Enough to dive to *zero* or soar to *zenith*.
M turned up *masturbation*, synonymed with

"Self-pollution." Pollute? What for? Who would?
But yearnings named under **H**, I understood.

Alum of the OED and *American*
Heritage, can I resurrect those teen

Cardings of the word-hoard's fibrous strands,
Sonic heirloom for today's string bands

That wire and text their lyric warp and woof
On *Explorer*'s Worldwide Web? Here's partial proof

That bedside ark, no tub or leaky dud,
Offered warm shelter in the mounting flood,

Where Noah housed his couples, aardvark, zebu,
And—I think unpolluted—my kind, too.

Letter to Marilyn Hacker

Marilyn, quick-witted author of poem-epistles, I trust you
Won't mind receiving one, drafted and sent with affectionate wishes.
Willing but hesitant, writers take up a new genre or subject,
Swearing they'll ditch it if stalled—or if soundings discredit the channel.
Didn't we say that the patron of meter's most likely Saint Rita?
Mother and guardian, vet these hexameters' dactyls and spondees!

First off, a grateful salaam for companionship during my visit.
Paris with you as accomplice was bracing and new—like the day we
Walked up to Belleville, *flâneurs* on a boulevard Walter
Benjamin's gold-rimmed bifocals must on occasion have X-rayed.
Yet, since the Twenties, worlds have collided, and strong multi-ethnic
Pressures have reshaped that neighborhood. Jews from Tunisia, Chinese,
Gallic *Français*, and Maghrebis from most of North Africa live there.
Barring a few minor set-tos, they seem to be getting along, while
Minding their shops and own business, a model of urban accord. So
Skeptics can't call you "utopian" once they assimilate Belleville's
Live affidavit that differences *don't* always turn into armed camps.

Next on the docket came Quai de Jemmapes, the Canal calmly trundling
Waters a subtle tint chemists once termed "Paris green." Leafy plane trees
Planted at one end provided a shade we abandoned for sunlight,
Opting to cross the arched bridge farther down. At the top of which we paused,
Charting the prospect like trekkers, like Aragon's *paysans de Paris*.
Just at that moment a barge on its way to the lock passed beneath us,
Marking its progress with sinewy furrows. Detritus of some sort,
Subfusc, anonymous, bobbed there, remember? An incident Henry
James once described in a letter resurfaced: How, when his friend Constance
Fenimore Woolson had plunged to her death from a window in Venice,
He'd been recruited to help with arrangements. What fell to his lot was
Distributing all of her gowns. But, instead, he decided to "drown" them—
Where but in *Canale Grande*, the smartest expatriate address? Black
Laces and histories darkened as each was slipped overboard. Weirdly,
None of them sank, they all floated. He sat in his gondola, silent,
Stricken. . .

A story that sounds like a fable, but what does it mean? Who
Knows? I don't. Meanwhile, that flotsam we noticed has washed away, vanished. . .
Besides, this is working-class Paris, not Venice of yesteryear. You turn,
Breathe, and suggest we push on. Future memories wait for adoption:
Take that new line of the Métro, which starts at the Madeleine, then six
Or possibly seven stops later concludes at the Bibliothèque François
Mitterrand, *i.e.*, the National Library. Proust I assume would
Smile at that—Mallarmé, too, since he said that the world was designed to
End as a book. Which makes sense if we add that a book (I mean good ones)
Will backslide, emerging as world-stuff or "life" once again. As your own do,
Marilyn—poet, American, francophone homegirl in Paris,
Recentest torchbearer in the tradition of Gertrude and Alice,
Natalie Barney, Renée Vivienne, Djuna Barnes, Janet Flanner,
Updates of *Liberty Storming the Barricades*. Sometimes the right wing
Tries to disparage a vocal progressive—which need not concern one
Whose manifest excellence writers and readers in several countries
Honor. Lutetia smiles, and her diadem sports a new brilliant.

Audubon

Early America's gone, extinct like the passenger
Pigeon, skies once an avalanche of migration
Now vacant but for clouds and vapor trails, the rare
Vector of bleating Canada geese, or a lone mallard.
And the land below laid bare, its forests cut and burned,
Demoted to tarmac, to strip malls and gated suburbs.

When ancestors at seven removes paused to scan
The green wild, impassable except where pierced
By trails non-natives couldn't scout, they guessed
More than was sayable about the unsurveyable,
And their own intrusion trivial. Audubon differed.
Subduing the awe reconnaissance stirred in him,
He leaned on his rifle atop the sharp promontory,
And indreamed a misted river valley grown vocal
With piped solfege from the birds of America.

Brushstrokes of oil or wash won their idea.
Taut silk feathers extended a fan to grasp buffeting
Updrafts, a shot taken on the wing, one gape-staring
Fish cramponed in airborne rapture, nature's tandem
Food chain captured and shipped to the Royal Society.

What he couldn't send was context—limitless terraces
Of air, the woodlands slip-knotted with vine and briar,
Creeks rich with tannin, the crossfire gaze of bear and cougar,
Scats, a ribcage stripped clean by crook-necked scavengers,
Insurgence of mosquito tribes, ponds paved with lilies,
A singular glycerine pearl affixed to each veined disc.
Epochs that saw the uprush of aeronautic tribes
Filmed in mirroring watercolor are passed and gone.
A wilderness, a fauna, erased. Not banished, vanished.
It won't return, or not until we go. Passengers.

In-Flight Couplets Composed During a Bomb Alert

London-St. Petersburg, August 14, 2006

Mind, though they've banned material counterparts,
Your conscious page and pen got past the guards.

Think back to Mandelshtam at the Black Sea,
Composing silently, invisibly. . . .

"It must be memorable." Yes, or else
Our uninscriptions will unwrite themselves.

Then, too, if bombs incinerate this brain,
It won't recall so much as my own name.

Exile, silence, equal oblivion?
Ask Mandelshtam. His *Tristia* may have been

The only book an author ever wrote
Each word of which the beloved got by heart.

Words fade to black if not made memories of.
Love, if it means to live, is spoken love.

Brodsky at the Caffé Dante

A Village den, not far from Morton Street,
Where you'd hosted a party just the week
Before, your birthday cake a replica
Of *A Part of Speech*'s jacket. A practical
Joke? It wasn't your most recent book,
Which blunt reviews had sort of trounced. But luck
'S a weathervane, and that year mine, too, had
Gone south, or sour, as I could tell you'd heard.

Strange: your large-scale forehead (the temple sported
A windswept curl Romantically borrowed
From Pushkin or Chateaubriand) was unlined,
Free of the trenches that gulags make or, exile.
Instead, it beamed a dynamic melancholy
Over our topics—none of them dire, really.
Ovid more vulnerable than Mandelshtam;
What Byron felt when he saw Dante's tomb.

I asked if you linked the San Marco Lion
To the address on St. Marks Place, where Auden
Had lived for decades. Just to hear his name
Unpacked a smile. . . In fact, the piece of cake
They'd cut you featured the King of Cats' brown sugar
Wing. Piston thrusts from that small figure,
Were counterparts to espressos we would drink—
Its caffeine still buzzing, I like to think.

HEREFORD

Heifers' doleful lowing out in the wolds.
So blithely blue a sky and clean a light.
Sweeter arguments for design than most,
They've also unearthed flashbacks of thatched eaves
Maybe one gentle rise (and another life)
Over from here, how many burnt sheep ago.
Byword in weather's local dialect,
A shower has blown up to cut the deal
For those who gambled on being here, afield
And downwind dove-gray, low-flown nimbostratus,
Natural speech a-lolloping a spray
Of welcome, your humble servant mac-less to boot.
Stranger, confess. Some deep-dug atavism
Spurred your recurrence here in parts remote.
Well, yes. . . And what if they should now say, "Stay"?

Fútbol

As if to move a flexible sphere from here
to there with unassisted head and foot
were natural and obvious. As if
a dance could always bow to resolute
constraint and never be danced the same way twice.
As if whistles and cheers, the hullabaloo
of fervent gazers were all the music needed
to keep its players' goals in tune. So that
as they weave, dodge, collide, collapse in breathless
haystacks—and rise and fall and rise again—
we're made, if not one, then at least whole.

Hadrian

Ambition even vast finds its limit.
But love goes undefined, a threshold crossed
As often as the passage serves to deepen
Hushed petitioners who falter toward
A torch-lit audience with the oracle.

Barricades that dammed back Caledonia
And its warriors also bridled the Empire,
Rome in its silver age a hub less driven
To centrifugal expansion via paved
Routes designed to spin out cohorts of shields
By the bronze, obedient ten thousand.
Standardized blocks constructed Caesar's rough-cut
Nec plus ultra, his full stop in stone.

A calculated number of leagues south,
Great Juno drifted into indolence.
The drowsy scepter slipping from her grasp
Clattered on tile and rolled toward the feet
Of a supple Ganymede from Greece
Who decanted an unstinting Hellenism
For the imperial eagle that had taloned
Him aloft. Dawns when light spilled over
Their tousled couch and lip met softer lip,
Northern troops with matted hair and bodies
Daubed black or red or white with crisscross signs
Glared at the horizon's show of offensive
Ramparts and raised a forest of roaring spears.
Blue chieftain eyes locked on the stoop of a hawk,
Hailed it, and exulted: "Rome will fall!"

But not yet. Hadrian bowed anointed curls
To his calyx of Falernian and drank
Their future, unaware the gods predestined
An Egyptian river whose warm genius would
Enfold and waft away the drowned cupbearer,

A mutable ephebe all seven hills
And loyal provinces agreed to mourn.

Less a ruin now than breached and broken
Stonework is, their eclogue's subscribed in full,
Bearded and beardless actor a dialogue
In the flickering amphitheatre
Where incident and passion, distilled as fable,
Manage not to drown in history.
They approach, take hands, embrace, and breathe a name.
When Caesar steps from loosened Tyrian robes
And youth lets fall its chlamys, not even empire
Outweighs the body's marble capital.
Cold centuries of sentries pace the wall,
Leaving it at last to midnight's legions,
The diamond surveillance of the northern stars.

Letter to James Fenton

James, transposing the stock opening
in which letter-despatcher invites
a friend to dinner, let me begin
with thanks for lunch at Long Leys Farm—and
for coming to fetch me at the steps
of the Ashmolean in Oxford.
Details will by now have blurred a bit:
When we drove up, from your door Darryl

emerged, epitome of soft-voiced
intelligence provided with skills
to manage a buoyant reunion
after I'm guessing more than five years.
Since you had a meal to assemble,
he volunteered to pilot my tour
of the grounds, first to their wilder part,
a pond where . . . herons?—yes, splashed and dove.

Beyond that, an Audenesque pylon,
modernizing the rural *laisser
aller*. And here the garden proper,
room after thick-petaled, leafy room,
rain-soaked annuals, perennials,
shrubs and trees, the plant kingdom given
a path to expression fresh enough
to leave me speechless. Talk resumed, though,

when I met your gardener and saw
how diligence could implement plans
an envisioner dreams and lays out.
Double capability, meanwhile,
had called us to a light, tasty lunch.
My topic: the morning spent in Prints
and Drawings, holding pen-and-ink works
by Samuel Palmer—among them

the age-twenty self-portrait in tan
and olive wash with gesso highlights.
Was it resolve or innocence that
spurred him to ponder wells reflecting
a hurt so much in earnest? And then
disclose what surfaced, youth's native gaze
conceived as elegy; and, in that
line, not surpassed by any artist.

More than most, James, you've been the poet
as traveler, appearing in "all
the wrong places," ironic Johnny-
on-the-spot for the fall of Saigon
and more gruesome junctures in recent
South Asian history. Now, after
a century of mass murders, how
to trump burnout if those listening

are too few to reverse the onrush
of disaster? I sensed world travel
no longer drew you, that you'd come home,
content to book passage on frigates
moored in your library. Couldn't they
hoist anchor straight off for classical
sites like *Animula Vagula*,
Ut Pictura Poesis, *Cras Amet*,

and current equivalents as well?
Call for imaginative passion
and you declare for justice also.
Beginning at the breakfast table:
distinct, low-key habits of *concert*
were discernible in that duo
I overheard, its reflexive poise
a moving contrast with the single
estate, or with partners less well matched....

Funny, I don't recall our goodbyes;
which probably would have been succinct.
But pictures so clear remain, it feels
as if I never entirely left.

Bond Street Station Underground

A fly-by cinematic apparition
Where window after sliding window past

Frames a supporting cast you never saw
Before—the student's dreadlocks spilling sidewise

When he laughs and bends his bearded grin toward
The girl with green tattoos and air-blue tube top—

The older person in widowed taupe, who blinks
At the tract her silver spectacles are trained on—

The City-bound executive with shiny
Pink tie and pin stripes angled at odd vectors—

A reddish fluff of curls and rope of pearls
That somehow match the surplus weight, say, "Flo"

Put on this spring when, what, her marriage ended.
She hefts herself up doorward, steps out slowly,

Glares at your stare. Unless you fancied her?
No. Or . . . Fresh blossom on a Maytime bough,

Lyrics once revered that now no longer
Reread you . . . . You leave them untouched. So what,

Get on, get on with it. But why? Because
You can't just stand there. Far away, in close-up,

They're filming us, and other eyes are watching.

Domus Cærulea

This sky afloat with cirri lacked a road map.
A Roman engineer called to survey it
Served eight summers, elated as a lover
All over again when handed new instructions.

Constructions as buoyant as desirable
Are able to hold in balance complex strains,
Extraneous yet consonant information.
Masons struck by Corona's starry chord

Record the constellation on a cork board
Covered now with green and light-blue pins.
Blueprints atop the tilted drafting table
Double the arc of love that lofted the dome,
The dominant harmonics an upraised
Appraisal of the day that lights our sky.

New England/China

Wakefield: Did some romantic alderman
Settle that name on our recycled mill-town?
I know Rhode Island is *Red* Island, or
Island of Roses. . . And, look, buds on Mother's
Haviland china, fifty years of attic
Storage ended, are pink, flushed with excitement
At being propped in ranks along the plate-rail
Of cabinets a shipwright made for this
Centenarian house I signed the deed on
Nine days ago. No way would I have served
Dinner on old porcelain in designer
Manhattan, my home turf for more than half
A prodigal life-span once I'd waved goodbye
To the South. But here it fits, a tasteful, gold-rimmed
Victorian replacement for the showy
Chinese export bowls and plates how many
Prosperous New England tables boasted
Back in the bullish age of clipper ships.
Those clashing pinks and reds epitomized
Spice roses of the Indies gunboats opened
To enrich our Union, sea to shining sea.

Following the *Vicar of Wakefield*'s homely
Advice, I've put a "Rose Medallion" teacup
(Bought for two dollars at a thrift shop) here
In this eastern window so its damasked pattern
Can go translucent as light rejuvenates
A naïvely rendered pride of mandarins
Hard at their silken round of tea and gossip
And poetry. The Vicar's older daughter
Olivia, the more romantic one,
Might have been charmed to join their circle, even
If her graver sister, Sophia, wouldn't want to.

Goldsmith, Mother most likely never read,
But *Gone with the Wind* she surely did and like

White Southern women of her day (except
The ambitious few who idolized Miss Scarlett)
Modeled herself on Melanie—for instance,
She never told black friends and workers they
Should "know their place" and stay in it. Her son,
If he works up his nerve, can copy her
(And risk a snub) by taking lemon pie
To the family next door, whose ancestry
Is African; and probably Narragansett,
Too, or else Pequot. Out beyond the teacup
I see their children, the older climbing up
On the garbage bin while holding an umbrella,
A taut silk octagon of alternating
Ebony and ivory pie-wedge panels
That read as either a black Maltese cross
Against a cream-white background, or a white
Against a black. She's poised to make her skydive
But seems to doubt the parachute; and none
Of her younger sister's urging turns the tide.
A pause, a balance; but she doesn't leap—
The Sophia of this family circle, just
As her wilder sibling's the Olivia.
Now their mother's called them to lunch, their game
Shelved with no decisions made, no plunge
Into the aerial realm of weightless pleasure.

I'll have my solitary codfish on
These resurrected roses—a chance to ponder
The leap I leapt in settling here and calling
The Ocean State, at last, the Golden Decades'
Ultimate Cathay. So, veteran frigate,
You, unlike the *Pequod*, may now dock
And prove that not all sexagenarians
Are skippers hot to tap-dance round the deck
Like Ahab, thirst for blood a scorching trade wind
That gives them forward thrust. The middle ground!
Vicarious pastimes, watching children's games
Or tending post-colonial and post-
Postmodern gardens, should amount to a sound
Retirement plan, Sophia, calm, deific

Wisdom, serving as hand-hewn figurehead
When our vessel comes to port. If goods we heft
Down the gangplank are only earthenware,
So be it, Yankees also favor those,
Judging from shards of broken plates and cups
I dug up planting the hybrid tea a friend
Gave me, the spot selected not haphazard,
Instead, exactly where a rose should go.
He laughed when told I'd named the house Knew Place—
A tribute to comedy's most tragic playwright.

But try to name or know a place you never
Lived in: Beijing. Nablus. Kabul. Baghdad. . . .
Imagination's olive branch stops short,
Absorbing the news that soldier and civilian
Sprawl face down in crimson pools enlarged
With all they owned, one clotting upshot of
Capitalism's abstract cannibalism.
Prosperity. Ours, but insubstantial,
Like all dream-castles based on greed, up there
Above the law. Who'd listen if I called
Our captains by their real names? They won't,
Conceded, but it doesn't seem to matter.
Out of the deeps, a voice: *Permission denied.*
No port for the tempest-tossed, you haven't yet
Begun to fight. Weigh anchor and make ready
For the clash. While you breathe, you won't retire.

Lighthouse

Pilot at the helm of a hidden
headland it steers free
from convergence with the freighter
when fog and storm clouds gather

Sparking communiqué no full stop ends
its broadcast sung in a three-sixty sweep
the cycle burning up five solar seconds

Midnight eye that blinks away
invisibility   a high beam
revealing as it scans whatever seas
or ships return terra firma's landmark gaze

UNIONS
(2014)

All It Is

The flexible arc
described by treetop leaves
when breathing currents ripple
a branch to one,
then the other side.
Or the level, quickened swell
that follows a gust over wetlands
home to a million reeds.

Any terrain you find arises from all
that came before: succeeding
event horizons from earlier eras
brought forward by today's considered
impetus to lift the way it looks,
lightly, freely
out towards whatever senses you are there—
breathed into completion, a sphere,
into all it is.

The Wall

I try and try not to think about the Wall.
Its profile, massive height and roughcut stonework
All stir up fear, gloom, exaltation, pride,
And numbness, in a jumble hard to name.

No one knows who had it built, or when;
Five hundred years ago, the locals guess;
But sunset trumpet calls depict it gold
Enough to have been there more than a thousand.

The thing held off invasions, true—but not
Always, our history records defeats.
Nowadays we never get invaders,
Or else they're us, going beyond its limits

To acquire new territory and subjects.
Though weaker stretches have sheared off and fallen,
Herders fence up their sheepfolds at the base,
And some blocks are dragged off to build new houses.

Topside, binoculars can sight its ramparts
Winding through dark-blue mountains farther north. . . .
That monumental, chill indifference
Explains why boys graffiti names on it

(Or jokes), no matter if their scrawny slashes
In time begin to erode. Decades ago,
I gouged in mine, it wasn't yet forbidden.
Luckily, dense vines screen the signature,

Made at an age when we assume our name
Amounts to more than permanent stone structures.
Oh, even now it sparks a vocal reflex
When I move the leaves and read it there again.

ELEVEN LONDONS

1967
Christmas carols, light-strings, mist, and rain.
Learning how to pronounce Marylebone.
A cut-rate holiday flight over the Channel
had lobbed us from our year on the Left Bank
to London, where Ann and I put up in a Baker Street
two-star, heated only when numb-fingered guests
fed shillings to the gas-gauge. Shillings, thruppence,
half-crowns, and the imaginary guinea:
Sterling's baffling component currency
had at least been marked down by Harold Wilson,
which gave grad-student cash a little boost.

Currency ruled, with birds on Carnaby Street,
rock fans at Camden Round House, the hip venue
for music happenings. Stones and under-thirties
were rolling their own, and soon as Jimi Hendrix
breezed into town youth hair ballooned out
in fluffy, copycat spheres. *Are you experienced?*
A purple haze drifted through Notting Hill,
compounded of smoke, incense and hallucination.
Fire up the time machine, get in and drive
with Vanessa Redgrave in *Blow Up*, levitate
on "Lucy in the Sky with Diamonds," and tune in
to visible autonomy now the overdue
Sexual Offences Act has gone into effect.

At Liberty's, my paisley shirt compared itself
to their extravagant flower-power cottons,
strawberry fields the Doors of Perception
could open on as before for Aldous Huxley,
Jim Morrison. And if for them why not for us?
Doors onto an innocence at least less vapid
than Holborn's fake Olde Curiosity Shoppe,
a private blamelessness we tried to fabricate,
making a separate peace untainted by what
America had locked, loaded, and fired in Vietnam

Sure, but innocence of the standard brand
won out when we queued up to see the Tower's
ravens, its tourist bait of regal finery.
With meeker if still jeweled exactitude,
Van Eyck's uncanny *Arnolfini Marriage*
wakened enlightened silence in the gazer,
transmuting a public-funded institution
into a Buddhist shrine for rag-tag pilgrims.

Our friend Jeanie guided us to Hampstead,
Keats' leafless garden persisting without his Bird,
a no-show we'd shrug off with a trudge up to the Heath,
to nurse a pint at Jack Straw's Castle, another
in the brown interior of the Spaniards—
somehow followed by a trip on the Northern Line
to Charing Cross and a prance down Whitehall,
the tall-hatted bobby on duty not bothering
to challenge whoever stepped into Downing Street.
So plant yourself in front of No. Ten's
unassuming door, take in the plain white spokes
of a fanlight set in soot-black brick, and then
push on to the bridge, waiting until Big Ben
strikes three, lit up by winter sun and brazen
as Hendrix's ax. Evening the same as morning,
Earth had not anything to show more. . . Cool.
We experienced the scene that experienced us,
reciprocal fuels pledged to set the night on fire.

1978
Yale English had opened its doors, to us
junior-faculty types, sufficient motive
for culling closer knowledge of the source.
At Paddington, no stereotype fogs
or rains, instead, mid-July heat. Reception
at our hotel in Bayswater suggested
Hyde Park as the guest's likeliest cool refuge.
Untrue in the event, but on we loped,
on past the statue of Peter Pan, recalled
from an album cover of *The Wand of Youth*.
My own I'd shelved; was serious; had published.
On offer at the National Portrait Gallery

were dour Tudors, Stuarts; Pepys, Blake, Shelley.
And why not follow up with a tiptoe through
Soane's lapidary house by Lincoln's Inn Fields?
Meanwhile, on the south bank of the Thames,
where, except to take in Turner's day-glow
cyclones, no one used to go, had risen
a massive modernist performance complex,
design triumphant in gray concrete.
                                                            Elsewhere
the Wallace Collection hoisted its genteel
standards, attracting patrons with Boucher,
or Poussin's *Dance to the Music of Time*, a title
Powell's panoramic Proustian twelve-speed
novel recycled for his own charmed circle.

1986
Planning to stay three autumn months, I lucked out
with a cheap flat on literate Gloucester Crescent.
I had some introductions: Adam M.-J.,
Marina W., and a Firbank expert
named Hollinghurst who worked at St. John's Gate,
the Clerkenwell base of the *TLS*.
Remarks he made were polite, forgettable;
but not the Jamesian glint in those brown eyes.

From my street, Regent's Park and its terraces
were an easy walk, and, in the opposite
direction, Camden Lock, where, Sundays, Euro
twenty-odds would flaunt their vampire getups.
Meanwhile, the newest London Library patron
ferreted out old curiosities
in St. James like Lock's, or Pickering Place, which once
sheltered an enterprising embassy
from the single-starred Republic of Texas.

In Spitalfields, the Dennis Severs house
relived its multi-generational stories,
level on level, not so far from Hawksmoor's
bone-gray neoclassical Christ Church,
a haunt fit for the Ghost of Christmas Present,
along with those that Jack the Ripper made.

And it was Dennis, monarchist as fervent
as only U.S. citizens can be,
who dragged me along to see the Royal Salute,
a show of cavalry and cannon-fire
staged in Hyde Park the festal day reserved
for the Opening of Parliament. When thunder
died down and smoke dispersed, we joined the hedge
of gawkers posted along the Mall until
Her Majesty's gold-leafed vitrine rolled past.
Kings may inspect a cat or commoner,
and for two public seconds our eyes met
across a revolving glove: I had been seen,
a disappointing spectacle, to judge
by the frown directed at my dark blue raincoat.

With Eliot as Baedeker, I found
The Waste Land sites—at least those not done for
in the blitz. Cannon Street and Lower Thames,
St. Mary Woolnoth, Magnus Martyr, Wren
inventions to burn, St. Mary le Bow, St. Bride's,
St. Mary Aldermary. HURRY UP,
PLEASE, IT'S TIME that Britain modernized
its slug economy, said the Iron Lady.
And, true enough, the City towers stood
to glass attention around the Monument,
a proud New Babylon that let the Blakean
handwriting crimson felt-tips had indited
on the Roman Wall go placidly unread.

Ed White dropped in from Paris, inviting me
for drinks at Le Caprice with Alan J.
and Nigella L., new talents I'd never heard of.
Redgrave stammered a harried Mrs. Alving
in *Ghosts*, and AIDS doom-saying filled the papers,
putting a pall on the singles scene. Connecting
became a new protectorate in need
of detailed diplomacy; which didn't mean
I stayed indoors and never danced at *Heaven*.
Didn't mean I failed to start a novel
with AIDS as a theme, the Cibber family
another. Research? Done beneath the beehive

dome of the Reading Room, at a desk Virginia
Stephen may once have propped her elbows on.

1987

If I meant that novel to conclude, I'd need
to come back for another stay. This time,
like a shimmering wand-waver out of Perrault,
Marina opened a door in Kentish Town
and set informal terms for a house let.
Rain sent down dark floods on the backs of brown
brick houses, over the chimneypots, spilled
from the pewter cloud cover. At Covent Garden,
Geraint Evans's farewell performance in *Falstaff*,
at the National, Judi Dench as Cleopatra.
Immortal longings, London in Thames melting. . . .
Slowly the expat metro-fiction settled
into focus, its goal, to fuse a travel
novel with history and match the clear-eyed
narrator with a certain place and era.
A city is a person; its votaries
read the Blue Guide's constellated pages
as a diary that keeps whole centuries
of the beloved's secrets. Which began
to include the latest love-struck resident.

1990

Arriving just at the pre-Christmas rush,
Chris and I found our three-star in Cartright Gardens,
my job to serve as volunteer Cook's tour.
Casting a cool eye on the horseman martyr
at the top of Whitehall, then the Banqueting House,
we paused at grillwork barring Downing Street,
closed now except to official visitors.
But Horse Guards hadn't changed at all, the off-white
tassels of their polished helmets dangling
in faces royalist, unblinking, handsome.

During dinner with D. and N., one wearing
red and black, the other, grape and green,
we heard that Spender's daughter was engaged
to an Aussie comic famous as "Edna Everage."

Had Auden at Christ Church been prescient, wondered
D., would he have failed to comment, "Stephen,
what you'll most likely end up being is
the married father of a daughter whose
husband is a brilliant drag performer."

Lunch next day at a Finsbury pub with Adam
and his new partner, a red-haired Scot from Skye,
both sporting motorbikes and leather jackets.
Intro reciprocity with Chris,
consensus beaming as if to say, "Well done!"

Scanning the West End, we'll veto *The Phantom*
in favor of *Three Sisters*, Redgrave's Olga
grasping at dimly foreseen straws of hindsight. . . .
As for music, Britten's rare *A Boy Is Born*,
performed in Smith Square, stars the holiday
we've been ignoring. Concert done, outside
we see a matron outstriding her plump husband,
who says, "Marie, I will *not* run!" That going
without effect, he hisses "Cat!". . . Old Possum's
lyrics sung on Shaftesbury Avenue,
the musicosmic comedy of time.

2000
Last week of the millennium. I'd been asked
to house-sit for D. and N. on Montagu Square
and to feed their Abyssinians, my only
company this visit. Single life:
hardly worth writing home about (*what* home?)
if change-of-scene pursuits cave in to gloom.
So I've listed dozens of must-sees like the new
Tate Modern down in Southwark, a giant hangar
in brown brick, reachable by a footbridge
built to commemorate the year, then closed
when traffic made it wobble. But you could still
arrive by tube to rubberneck at the hall,
a guest at the wedding of high-tech and art.
Faustus, begin thine incantations. . . Or don't.
Late afternoon the 31st, I noticed
embroidered mottoes on Westminster Abbey

altar cloths: *And all manner of thing shall be well,*
plus Eliot's *the fire and the rose are one.*

2002
Exiles themselves from Ethiopia,
the pets again accepted me as minder
while D. and N. spent a July in Paros.
(George Bush's jingoistic rap had made
expatriation more and more appealing.
Be careful, though. In today's hawkish climate,
vocal dissenters acquire a dossier.)

The newly stabilized bridge let me cross it
from Southwark to St. Paul's and find my chair
for Evensong, as sung, with no apparent
irony, for one of the ancient guilds,
The Worshipful Company of Ironmongers.
Next, Bottom and I would wince a long midsummer
night on the Globe's relentless oaken bench;
attend the ENO Purcell *Fairy Queen*;
and meet Marina at Kings Cross to hear
Barry's *The Triumph of Time and Deceit*—
as camp as modern opera can get
and not just float up to the flies. From Adam,
a glass of elderflower at his flat in Highbury,
and, next day, lunch with laughing Yvonne G.
in the Middle Temple's Great Hall, where colleagues
convened in her early years as a barrister.
I haven't verified *Twelfth Night* was once
staged there for Gloriana, so, will someone?
Outside, the old round church prompted a pause,
its Templars crossing long stone legs on tombs
engraved with Norman titles. But the Grail quest
faded when we made our way to Fleet Street.

Queen's Gallery: Vermeer, her portrait by Freud,
Carracci's *Trionfo del tempo e del desenganno*,
seen possibly by Handel, and then Barry?
From Marble Arch, I walked to Edgware Road,
its Mid-East flavor marked by outdoor shisha
cafés and news-racks stocked with *Al Jazeera*.

At the London Mosque, guards with walkie-talkies
stared long and hard at anyone approaching.

Chelsea solitudes, the Physic Garden laden
With Liberty-print wisteria, with rue and elder.
Acknowledge Thomas More's restored Old Church,
give Cheyne Walk its due, then on to Tite Street,
to find the plaque put up for Oscar Wilde—
and the Worshipful Company of the Yellow Book,
some of whom added their voices to that solemn
De profundis of the Oakum Picker.

2003
At the Greens' in Clifton Gardens, kind supports
for my overconfident intention of joining
D.'s months-long bedside vigil for poor N.,
once doctors said that no more could be done.
(In fact, I never got to make goodbyes;
or work through mourning for a Byzantine
intelligence that put heart first, lighting
the deep proscenium where fact meets vision.)

Yvonne read out new poems in the garden.
The children painted masks for Purim, stringing
paper chains above the kitchen. Then walked
to the old Spanish-Portuguese *shul* where
Esther's recited prototype foreshadowed
X number of eleventh-hour rescues.

The secular could stroll through Little Venice,
Regent's Canal a mooring for long barges
named *Esmeralda*, *Little Pud*, or *Rose*.
Tea at the Poetry Place near Covent Garden
with Mimi K., who spoke of childhood in
the "elfin" Isle of Wight. A matinee
of *Endgame* in St. Martin's Lane, the blindman
Michael Gambon's black lenses like punched holes
from which grim insight flowed as he raved and snorted,
till house lights rose and spectators filed out.

2005

Bush re-elected, I laid my plans to desert
a nation-state become coercive, Texan,
my substitute two smallish rooms in Hampstead—
perfect if you liked its Georgian-Euro
mix, the expelled Green Man reanimated
on rolling tracts of Heathside, semi-wild
woodland. Bags unpacked and books on shelves,
I hiked there over zebras, traffic islands,
to Jack Straw's Castle, which, revamped as modern
up-market condos, blared loud ads for buyers.
Unreal. A sigh, a plod to the famous view
for a telephoto fix on distant towers
below, including one nicknamed "The Gherkin."
Globalization. Passive resister seeking
asylum, where to now? Back to your lair.

Or to the Spaniards, its dim, snug allure
unchanged. To Adam, now living in Herne Hill,
for a meal with his (to me) new partner Keith.
Or a Kentish Town reunion with Marina,
her place redone, yet recognizable
as we puff upstairs and find a place to sit,
ticking off updates, good and less than that.
Oh, but there are instances when appeal
sidesteps attrition, the comedy of eyes,
nuanced verbality, deft, pared-down gestures. . . .

And does middle age whip up an appetite
for medieval surrounds? Falstaff knows,
so here, two decades on, is St. John's Gate,
the brick-and-limestone Charterhouse, Ben Jonson's
St. Bartholomew, and Cloth Fair Street,
where a pub called "Betjeman's" looks fresh and smart.
I took Sir John's collecteds from the Keats
Branch of the Camden Libraries, next door
to the ailing genius's beige house, bemused
when I heard *two* nightingales begin to wrangle.
Summoned by Bells sent me up to Highgate for
those footsteps, rustling leaves, the blackbirds arcing
down—afterimage of his *pre-war world,*

Where firelight shone on green linoleum.
In search of Blake's lost Heaven, a turn from
South Moulton onto Brook. And what springs up but
Hendrix's plaque, hard by the Handel House,
As Jimi—hallelujah!—married to
his Hell-bent lyrics, must have chuckled over.
"Paradise"? Revivified experience.
Sound out this theory at the renovated
London Museum, freshly recreated
strata of city chronicles retold
in unearthed bone and fired-clay artifacts.
Add Guild Hall, too, after the blitz rebuilt
with repro giants Gog and Magog perched
in its rear balcony, plus excavated access
to the Roman theatre deep underground—
a refuge from barbarians till Rome
called time, quit Albion, and scuttled home.

From our equivalent imperium,
a Christmas visit from Philip A., sparked up
with energies that Piccadilly's limber
bronze archer might claim partial credit for.
Remember the warm afternoon we hiked
to Parliament Hill and watched a fleet of kites
swirling their swoops, an animated paintbox
menagerie? I couldn't summon up
every detail about Dick Whittington's
fabled about-face maybe two miles north,
but sketched what scenes I could. Then, walking back
across that little bridge, a psychic reader
practiced at living in the future said,
"This will turn out to be another of
those unmomentous moments that for reasons
tricky to formulate you don't forget."
Dusk moved in from its eastern earliness,
black trees reflected topside down in water,
a peach-flesh glow suffusing the anti-twilight.

2006
I'm booked to give an Oxfam reading early
in July, with Philip coming over for

a sort of honeymoon. When Anne-Marie
and Cahal give us a meal in Bedford Park,
I recall that Jack and Willie Yeats once lived there,
emblems of a fluent expatriation
Kavanagh and a younger Eire revived.
Green leaves slow-dropping rain, fine Arts and Crafts
Houses, light in a turret window. . . But
we've got tomorrow's drive to Wales before us,
so have to make an early evening of it.

And back only a day before P's flight
when petrifying newsbreaks sound the alarm:
Police say British Islamists are planning
to blast eleven international
flights to Crusader's Hell. Cold panic jams
Heathrow where, detained for more than thirteen
hours after check-in, he at last
flies safely home. Which leaves me shaken, numb,
meandering the streets in a fried daze.
Casting around for some innocuous
mood-lifter, I remembered having often
postponed a visit to the Leighton House
in sedentary Kensington. Today, then?
The project sounded mild and should have helped
except that the most lavish of its rooms
evoked lush scenes from the *Arabian Nights*
or, closer home, the saga of T.E. Lawrence.
What Iznik tiles in blue, white, and blue-black
can do had been done, fitted to the high
ogees and tall faux mihrab opposite
one trickling fountain. Add a narghilé
and "Oriental" fantasies would have been
complete, if hard fact hadn't smashed them all—
along with the Aesthetic Era's fine
distinctions priests of art like Whistler, Swinburne,
and Beardsley drew, their pipe dreams pale and helpless
before philistinism's foursquare onslaughts.

2007
Eve of departure for the title city,
and Philip says his packing's almost done.

I'm reading Shelley's *Triumph of Life*, the lamp
throwing a warm, illuminated circle
on facing pages of a sixties edition,
complete with fragments like this late Dantesque
outcry. Fragments: Why did the Romantics
produce so many? Well, suppose that "life,"
the personal, transfixing avalanche
of innocent experience, ironic
triumphs, a stark, euphoric blend of cheer
and disappointment is itself the perfect
open-ended fragment. Which, though in-
complete, is something like our day job, vital,
current, the partly conscious estuary's
untrammeled, unacknowledged legislation
freighting its raw material to the mind.

A flight from Kennedy will snatch us aloft
for touchdown at Heathrow. From whose express
we'll watch repeat brick houses speed and darken
under fresh showers, then yield to stone and steel.
Let friendships rekindle, doors we know or don't
open on memories involuntary
or subpoenaed; read papers, absorb the fact
that recent changes in Common Law can marry
us if we need law to shore up commitment.

At last, midsummer light will climb back down,
a flushed Prime Minister resigning, his stage,
in this scenario, Westminster Bridge—
appropriate for drowning tools of office,
the river running softly with common parlance,
iconic echoes, summits, past addresses,
lines got by heart, cool voices rocking on
the sunset's red, resilient grave, not one
with any plausibility recycling
Shelley's sign-off: *'Then, what is life?. . . .'* In place
of the usual depressing blare of trumpets,
it leaves the run indefinitely extended.

In a Bottle

Sails hoist but stalling, this two-master
Galleon in its prison of glass
Nose-dives, seesaws on swells of fire,
Bowsprit the needle of a compass
Drawn upward first by a fixed star,
Then down by the blue hypnotic deep.

After months of wave onslaught and bluster,
The cork pulls loose, but now what tool
Will spring nonliquids from their trap?
No whale-road spied to let her rip,
The pent-up vessel's lulled by a cool
Woodnote fluted across the lip
While moorings in the portside distance
Call, call, with tormenting persistence.

Bob

For Mimi Khalvati

Why go? Partly because we had no reason
To, though, granted, Hastings's on the Channel—
Which meant salt air and, that day, winter sun.
A zigzag swing from station down to shingle

For inhaled gusts of light and arrowy
Jeers shrilled by veering scavengers overhead,
Who flirted, razzed, then flapped and rowed away,
Our tentative footsteps fumbling pebbles, dead

Shellfish, kelp, plastic bits. A backtrack trek
To lunch should keep mild melancholy at
Bay, even if the loose-ends, Fifties-flick
Ambiance was what we'd come for. Or part of what.

Later, our huff-puff climb uphill for the ruins'
Majestic overviews, in guidebook blather.
One silver path across the waves to France,
And the long, incoming roar of faith from farther

East. (Or west: fanaticism's viral.
Numbing to think about the human cost.)
Sunset. Time to unwind a dawdling spiral
Down to the mall—where it dawns on us we are lost.

Lost. Let's ask this sporty adolescent.
"The station? Oh, no problem. Bang a right
Up there, then left, and on along the Crescent
About two minutes, and Bob's your uncle, mate."

You smiled, interpreted—but then you *would*,
Having yourself once been an "alien."
(The conditional of ironic likelihood
Is hackneyed. Stop me if I use it again.)

Transit to London as night falls. First star.
Abrupt flashes of interrupting light
Light up your eyes, your lipstick, your shimmering hair.
Friend. Nothing more. . . . *And Bob's your uncle, mate.*

A Free Translation

Transatlantics any length of time
In London learn to call them *trainers*, not
"Athletic shoes"; and instead of "tic-tac-toe,"
To compete at *noughts and crosses*; meanwhile taking
The *underground* or *tube* and not the subway
(Which here's a tunnel over there we call
An "underpass"). So passing under one
Today I surged up to the din and traffic
Of Oxford Circus, an overpopulated
Transport snarl that felt just like Manhattan.

Let Hamlet cross the *zebra* and *work out*
Just why he doesn't *carry on* speaking *Yank*.
Gormless of me? Some sort of verbal homage
To a granddad born and bred in Liverpool?
Or to the quirky parlance of the help
We had back when, and her readiness to praise
People "whose understanding wasn't nought."
The local terms are second nature now,
So I'll just *muck in* and translate myself,
As I do on trips to Paris, speaking French.

Parrots and copycats come in for satire,
And yet last month I heard a young Dane croon
In, what, Nashvillian?—specifically,
With Neil Young's voice, a country twang that wouldn't,
Even for us, be all that easy to master.
And Jessye Norman's German's as convincing
As Renée Fleming's when-in-Rome Italian.
Loping on, caught up in *flâneur* thoughts,
I'm crossing over to the South Bank now,
The feet department holding up. *Press on*, then,

The **OXO** Tower my beacon, with its match
Of noughts and crosses only just begun.
"Divided by a common language." And,
Since what divides things joins them too, united.

Dublin Night

Roving packs you eel your way
through pay no mind to what must, if they see,

look like a shadow loping along alone,
now slowing, stopping for the misted warmth

etched panes suffuse in the Hound and Rose's matched
bilateral doors. Ale glow that lights up half

of the fatman's baldpate football head,
left paw cupped to his mobile ear,

the splayed right cranking up and down
as his tenor wades alive-o into the rant.

Leave him behind then for that mid-bridge figure
(my body double?), more than half involved

with swirls and frills of foiled reflections
on the black stream coursing under. . . .

A water no less cold than cash, it will
or will not clutch him to its heaving silk.

In the Grünewald Café

Where do slackers go to get their jollies?
Where do they spend hours every day?
Where commit their most moronic follies?
In the Grünewald Café.

The dull-eyed types who sit alone? They're boozers
Who dose their coffees with Grand Marnier.
No one ever tells them they are losers
In the Grünewald Café.

You hadn't seen the mobster's girlfriend. Tasty,
But are you sure her goon has gone away?
It's not so wise to come on overhasty
In the Grünewald Café.

You sidle up and say, "Can I get you a drink?"
She's shuffling cards and seems to want to play.
A smile means "Try your luck, guy," don't you think,
In the Grünewald Café?

Card game done, why not get down to cases?
Up close her blue-green eyes seem less blasé.
All around you fools are pulling faces—
In the Grünewald *Café*?

Yet when your hands touch, someone taps your shoulder.
It's the waiter: "Sorry. Care to pay?"
A silence falls. Things suddenly feel colder
In the Grünewald Café.

The red-faced gangster, packing heat, approaches.
A rod's blunt business end. You start to pray.
What made you hang out here with all these roaches
In the Grünewald Café?

How brief it is, that fiery burst of thunder!
Brief as life, brief as a winter day.
To croak because you made a stupid blunder
In the Grünewald Café!

And now this floating view down from the ceiling:
Blood soaks the spot where your dead body lay.
What song, what words express all that you're feeling?
In the Grünewald Café.

Cascade of Faces

Five seconds of fame drag them down
the screen, ranks, names, faces, ages:
Staff Sergeant Hannah Nagel, 24.
Private Tom Abeel, 19.
Major Luís Moreno, 33.
Lance Corporal Rafiq Ibrahim, 20.
Captain Roger Kean, 31.
Candid American faces, unblinking,
unafraid, unvenal, snapped
a year, two years ago, not yet reviled
or revered, the newscast's evening crop.

Images swallowed up, transfigured,
launched into an unlived future.

*

On the Oval Office desk,
dead center, one hot white spot
lights the briefing's final page.
A chief executive is working late,
behind him, tall windows onto
a sky petroleum black,
strewn with trembling sparks.

*

In another hemisphere noon towers over
a desert city where his signature ignited
hair, skin, and eyes of the unknown civilian.
One by one, for how many terrorized
hundred-thousands the precedent was set,
roofs, walls, thundering down on their screams.

*

He reaches to snap out the lamp, ambles
to a door that closes on his steps.
Official darkness. Clockwise stellar bodies,
in their long-term impartiality, continue
rinsing the blackboard,
rinsing the blackboard—
which in a decade, or a century,
will free itself from any obligation
to save a chalked-up tally of the cost.

The Great Pessimists

Vanity of vanities. . . There is no remembrance of
former things;
Nor remembrance of things that shall be with those that shall come after.
—Ecclesiastes

And yet Diogenes still roams the world, lantern in hand,
An exodus in search of honesty, his greeting to Alexander:
"Stand aside, you're blocking my sunlight."

And the prophet who lashed out, "The heart is
Deceitful above all things, and desperately wicked.
Who can know it?" Lear could, we hear it in his howls,
Or Gloucester's "as flies to wanton boys are we
To'th gods, They kill us for their sport." Or Macbeth,
His candle snuffed, a walking shadow, a ham actor
Full of sound and fury, significance's zero sum.

Apostle of mordancy, ironic La Rochefoucauld,
Who detected self-regard in every generous act,
Reasoning that reason always proved the dupe
Of emotion. And that we could no more control
The tenure of our passions than the duration *vanity*
Of our lives. Asserting that, when a friend had suffered
Setbacks, some part of the mind was not displeased.

And Schopenhauer's "Every man takes the limits
Of his own field of vision for the limits of the world."
None possessed energy enough to hate every fool
Encountered—but despise them all? Nothing easier.

And Freud's obit for the declining West, its chronic
Bloodlettings, based on indelible discontent.
His goal: to dispel neuroses' aching fogs
So that his patients might face the incurable
Dread that conscious flesh cannot escape.

Eliot's rootless dilettantes and psychics,
His prickly pears, flickering rodents and shattered
Glass; who said we should be grateful for human
Ignorance and folly, as our only insight
Into the nature of infinity. . . .

Or Kafka's bewildered quester, an insect scrabbling
Through labyrinths of spite and muddle, the mind's cavern
Echoing with paternal scorn, hurled judgments
Not to be separated from the Creator's own.
And when They confirmed your guilt, you "died like a dog."

Or Beckett's bedraggled, bleary clowns, tatterdemalion
Down-and-outs nattering on in some vague terrain a bit
Off the phrenological map. Three walls do of the stage
A prison make, ourselves the fourth, bogged in our lusts,
Ambitious for more life, more pelf, more dust.

Each morning a featherless biped buttons up its layers
Of plotted insulation so as not to (or let others) see
The preened banality of practical defenses.
A vacuum, a simulacrum lays down the foundation
For achievement, hollowing out the moment of arrival
On some plateau where reptiles in chain-mail slither
Through abandoned quarries and a rasp abrades the air:
Nothing puts an end to emptiness but nothingness.

Common Dwelling

Mornings, early, others make themselves
at differing levels heard and even felt,
at least, if you can guess the gist
of another life from sound alone.
Like the enviable neighbor couple
who shift and stir less than an arm's length
behind the headboard, their murmurs
sifting into consciousness
as though no sheetrock intervened.
It's the sonic ambient for one last
underwater, shut-eye scenario,
which holds until the alarm starts prodding.

Downstairs, would that be a he or she
who in pre-dawn gloom grinds french roast
for the day's first espresso?
And not just once but vibrantly again
after what must be a caffeinated interval.
Alertness has its downside, though,
delivering this thought: the practice
of selfhood turns into an addiction.

Heavy boots not muted by rugs clunk
about on the floor above. Months
of obstinate slogging guarantee
their pace would instantly anywhere
be recognized, if not the pacer.
Odd moments in the day he launches
his campaign with a ruckus that feels
coercive, sure, but on behalf of what?

No choice *but* tune in when an amped-up
boom of heavy metal from across
the landing detonates after nightfall,
puffs of cover-up sandalwood incense
stealing in under the door. Nirvana:
who knew that howls would signal its arrival?

Hi's or *goodby-I-love-you's* ring out
every time a door opens, then slams,
but the cocked ear can't detect either
sequels or concluding flourishes.
Our hive's improvisations amount
to a sound track, hum and buzz
emerging from angular cells
hospitable to the general detachment.

Or think of it as a single body, limbs
and nerves sending bulletins
to the brain bent over its clipboard.
Overloaded, dutiful, the thing wonders
what to do with this daily repeated
and recklessly partial information.

Interior Florida

1.

Lamplight. Outline of a drowsing figure
slumped in the black mirror
that has supplanted HD color
shoot-outs and recipes a remote
switched off some dozen breaths ago.
Think of offbeat cinematic shots
targeting the actor from inside
a hearth, a medicine chest, a freezer.
And that Ibo proverb: *When the moon*
is shining even the lame man longs for a walk.

Midnight wants a refill—music, say,
in liquid form. But someone else's malaise
begins to wash in, its transparent emblem
a crescent trembling in the tumbler tilted
towards attention that thirst makes keener.
Raise a toast to their FM program,
onrushing tonal scenarios broadcast
live, it sounds like, from another state.
State, or not yet defined destination,
the region half in shadow that borders this one.

Footsteps barely audible, a fable
comes moiling up the stairs. Second-story
man, with Luger cocked?
No, it's just arthritic Mrs. Atropos,
Who's clocking in without her sisters,
hand cupped around the candle flame,
an orange glow undergirding her face.
The same beldam who rinsed a plate, arranged
flowers, and with no apparent reluctance
applied her shears to tight-stretched lifelines
when the destined year and day came up.

Clean vacancy never waits long to be
stained with event, intention: a white plate,
and on it, blood-red tomatoes, each with a wiry
green starfish attached where stem meets skin.
Resemblance modulates to undertow,
its impetus in retrospect outdistanced
by a hundred million evolving years,
tumbled breakers pitching forward, lurching
on all fours towards the shore, slowing, pausing;
then sluiced back seaward to make a new assault,
scaly coldbloods run aground and by some nameless
telos compelled to move, move, move,
though only the fittest thrash on and continue,
originators of a species.

Look down a well eons deep. It's petrifying.
So at last detachment collapses the telescope,
cuts to an environ whose sundry includes
wheelchairs, clocktowers, asters, squirrels
streaming across a lawn strewn with maple leaves—
the parti-colored field of the visible
with no sharp sense of when a "now" begins.

2.

Memory as a police procedural. During that tenth summer, eager for sea air, we drove to Florida, one week after V.'s first birthday. She fidgeted or blinked or slept on Mama's lap. The tropics: palm and orange tree, bougainvillea, oleander. A breeze from the Gulf and its sands. Black men and women on a park bench fanning themselves. Roadside table selling local corn and tomatoes. Our radio picked up a classical station—not that I knew the term "classical music." Along with high pings sung out by circling mosquitoes and the offended wails of the baby, something reticent, a sound texture fateful and achingly gentle unspooled itself into the car interior. On the crest of an indrawn breath, thought stopped. Timid, unencouraged, the second-youngest comes close to asking what the piece was. But of course they wouldn't know. During our return trip, one miles-long contrail against submerging solar fires cleared the stage for a dramatic moonrise, Florida's enormous darkroom developing its pictures.

An education later (one scrap of evidence), I matched those sounds to the name "Mozart," no doubt one of his symphonies, but which? Nor is anything cleared up by juxtaposing its orchestrated inwardness and V.'s death, ten days after our drive. She had somewhere contracted spinal meningitis; and didn't recover. Long before experts had coined the term "survivor's guilt."

Tropisms, tracks, godots. . . .

The unreflective play to win,
a game plan epidemic or endemic,
though chances are they'd call it backbone.

Where but else, in this accelerated future
clarity that wants to call up the castaway
spun under walloping ceilings of combers
massed offshore, a headlong inertia that wakes only
when surfacing breath releases its own broadcast
gasp, the remote chance of survival granted,
even if granted selectively,
even if, in their unconscious, infant
existence, things break off
mid-dissonance, without—

Wait. Sound alert. A groundswell of modulating
chords, one fine thematic thread floating
in rose-gold skies above them.
The beforemath, and then a minimal
finale. Silence. The work now
identified. Its second movement. Adagio.

That was the one. That's it. The very same.

I guess they won't, tonight, perform the third.

Best Is Never to Be Born, and If Born. . .

But those who plan to live till they are old
Consider it failure if, while young, they die.
The mountains of the moon are parched and cold.

We don't know what age means, we aren't told.
Too kind to speak, grandparents smile and sigh
For those who plan to live till they are old.

Eroded tendons and joints no longer hold.
Which will go first, the weakening ear or eye?
The mountains of the moon are parched and cold.

Formulas, tonics, pills and creams are sold
To halt the steep decline. Ads never lie
To those who plan to live till they are old.

Donne didn't send to know for whom they tolled,
The passing-bells. Who doubts what they imply?
The mountains of the moon are parched and cold.

Be careful what you wish for. Rainbow gold
Withers into mere reality.
For those who plan to live till they are old,
The mountains of the moon wait, parched and cold.

Cementario Recoleta

Buenos Aires

Stasis at noonday. *Carnaval.* Past stately palms,
Near the entrance, a "living statue," in red-embroidered
Cloth-of-gold robes and hat, the stolid, sweating face
A grease-paint icon, parasol unfurled against
Carcinogenic light. His wooden begging bowl

Takes your dropped coin, admission to a Shadowland
Inside whose gate each new arrival scans a map
To ground the mute dream-kingdom's myth and keep it real.
Mute? No, dead, in vaults hermetically sealed,
Lined up like ranks of books awaiting their great Critic.

"Lugar de mi ceniza,"[1] In fact, a false prediction.
He's not here in some marble palace with Greek columns
And bridal angels, not here among gray obelisks
And patronyms that also name the Centro's broad
Avenues: *Saenz Peña, Sarmiento, Lavalle.*

Which is better, to end as shrine, or road? A granite
Beaux Arts pavilion, or a capital's frenetic,
Polluted throughway? Cool, unruffled by the question,
Veteran arbor vitae branches breathe and nod,
Liquefying shade on this stone bench. Be seated,

Released from gravity and able to unburden
At a crossroads in the garden of forking paths where birth-
And death-dates tie their knot and so remind us living
Statues we never can know where or when the golden
Eulogies will rain down on us like palmfuls of earth.

---

[1] *"Place of my ashes"*: In his poem "Recoleta," Jorge-Luis Borges predicts his future interment in this cemetery, though, in the event, he wasn't buried there.

Poe Lucifer

The daylong dive of that aggrieved archangel:
Only those who've known defeat can fathom
Him, when he drops headlong from the ramparts—
Slippery rim of the abyss, engulfing
Wings of a vast nocturnal bird of prey,
The Morning Star's dismemberment of mind.
Anarchy's ruins, its fading trumpet calls,
Somehow evoke, when they become reflective,
A city's darkened towers beside the water.

A city's darkened towers beside the water
Somehow evoke, when they become reflective,
Anarchy's ruins, its fading trumpet calls.
The Morning Star's dismemberment of mind?
Wings of a vast nocturnal bird of prey,
Slippery rim of the abyss, engulfing
Him when he drops headlong from the ramparts.
Only those who've known defeat can fathom
The daylong dive of that aggrieved archangel.

Hunting Season

A quick tap on the barometer and in roughly ten seconds its pointer will turn to the word that names prevailing atmospheric conditions, low or high, the former paradoxically implying the approach of a storm. Low. Yet the view out the window couldn't be calmer. A man walking along with his dog, white with irregular patches of russet, a completely likable, strokable animal that suddenly freezes, left front paw lifted and tucked, muzzle aimed at the gamebird in hiding. Not shouldering a rifle, with no visible interest in the hunt, the man continues along, his dog ambling after, the hidden game keeping to its bolt-hole. A complex piano piece on the radio abruptly shifts into a quiet chorale-like passage with no counterpoint at all, just vertical and modal harmony. Gooseflesh, and it feels as though I've just remembered afternoons long gone and forgotten, something ancient, events unfolding centuries before I was born. I can almost reach it. In orange sunset light, I'm alone, walking, woolgathering, with deserted plains and hills stretching out ahead. Jolted when I approach a sign with an eastward arrow saying TIRANA, ONE THOUSAND MILES. Something like that. When the passage ends, I'm catapulted back into the present, restored to the normal stress levels generated by daily life in this speeded-up age. *Sturm und Drang*: I'm overstating, and yet here it comes, a pointed commentary on this moment, black clouds, winds, flailing branches, two pheasants exploding into the first downward scattershot raindrops. Sing, goddess. Lightheaded, I'm ready to be torn apart.

Perfect Pitcher

for David

The invaders used a non-vegetarian method
of emptying the town of its populace.

What we see is a kind of *attributed* trembling, as
with stars, or pebbles in the streambed of a brook.

He led us a dance, which ended in closed-mouth laughter.
A brimming fountain in the middle distance spilled like a willow.

The poem misses, and only by a
hairsbreadth, being nothing but itself.

Windowframe. Branch of a red maple
bowing before the breeze, seventeen times.

Don't call that cerise shirt "loud." Colors
have feelings too, they can hurt, same as words can.

Over a tall glass J. and I babbled
of green tables and W.C. Fields.

Travel time backwards far enough, and you'll see
sweetness is as unterrible as poured milk. Concentric

echoes in the pond console the lost beloved's image.

Möbius Strip

An unexpected lithe half-turn, his corkscrew
torsion back and around to lock gazes,
the vibe that jolts us awake just as surprising—
so . . . obstinate? so shaken—where some four
or five inrushing attitudes competed.

I wondered if any but a wrestler's waist
and neck could helix up to exhibit
the blush, the cool resilience of a face
still damp from a hot shower, and maintain
our stable dovetailed tempo further down.

Espresso ringlets tangled over blue-green
eyes bracketed to one side like a film star's,
jaw clenching, and no routine f-word needed
to convey the ache, the angry exultation
that can't help being selfish when it feels good.

OK, my chuckle's too much of a gloat,
so you lean back for a snog that shuts me up,
teamwork teasing the brink until one vaulter
arcs and plunges earthward. . . . Left behind,
all right, but no complaints from this postponer.

As both sides of our bodied Möbius
strip become each other, you'll soon be seeing
me make my half-turn, trusting to meet your gaze.

Lily of the Valley

The flower in French called "muguet"
Thrusts up from woodland beds in May,
Its mini-steeple's carillons
Tolling their scent in cool green tones.

Though dozens of springs have flared and fled,
I'll leave the number unstated.
Buoyantly vague, it will weigh less
Than nature's early timelessness.

Our lifespan has been termed "a vale
Of tears." Yet a dry word might prevail
On this *Fleurs du mal* memento thing
To breathe and say what's happening.

Swiss Army Knife

The first weighed light dense heavy in my palm
back in the days when Ann and I'd go trekking,
stalking the wild asparagus. Two blades,
can-opener, screwdriver, toothpick, auger—
all stowable in one sleek plum-red case
emblazoned with a logo silver shield
that bore the foursquare cross of Switzerland.

Lost, at what point in that decade, unknown.
I rummaged, searched and—not there. Stolen, maybe.
Plotting its zigs and zags, time cuts both ways.

Well, one such knife's much like another; its blithe
replacement could have almost duped the wielder.
Repertory stretching as years raced by,
we learned to clean a grubby nail, to pop
a cork, and (if not always those I hoped for)
to open letters—some with compliments
phrased for eyes that read between the blades.

Next time I *could* cite theft—of the overnight
satchel that Chris had packed it in, at least.
Rage a hack might describe as blind or stabbing
slid in between adjacent ribs. So did I
march off again to find a duplicate?
Mm-hm, but chose instead a variant
in black, the unfathomable color favored
by mourner, artist, urbanite, and priest.

Guru, to keep acumen fresh you seldom
sally forth and only then with core
safeguards. Second guesses, disapproval?
No, but I've heard your thoughts: "Today's a salt
synonym for all that is. Walk softly,
gaily. This compact, black-and-silver ally
will throw the story into strong relief
and lend an edge to years that came before."

Closing Night

Curtain. Our set, one last time struck by helpful
Assistants staggers, topples, and impacts
With a thunderclap. Snap goes the silver bell-pull,
Table and chairs upend, a large bowl cracks.

Fourteen weeks, and *The Party*'s over. Wakened
From its fever dream, dramatis personae
Sloughed off, we move stage front for a goodbye
Heartfelt as only practiced skills can make it.

Bit parts drift up to offer comic relief,
Promise to be in touch, to meet for lunch.
We exchange fibs as spotlights fade, and laugh
When darkness floods the house, the worn red plush
Still warm from fans who'll want an autograph—
Signed quickly, as, "perforce," we must be brief.

MUSIC OF EXPERIENCE

Life's brass, percussion, keyboard, winds and strings
Inflect the silence of eternity.

Alfred Corn has published eleven books of poems, two novels, and three collections of critical essays. He has received the Guggenheim fellowship, the NEA, an Award in Literature from the Academy of Arts and Letters, and one from the Academy of American Poets. He has taught at Yale, Columbia, the University of Cincinnati, and UCLA. In 2013, he was made a Life Fellow of Clare Hall, Cambridge. In 2016, Chamán Ediciones in Spain published *Rocinante*, a selection of his work translated into Spanish, the same translation appearing the following year in Mexico under the title *Antonio en el desierto*. He has published translations from classical Greek, Latin, French, German, Italian, Russian, Chinese and Spanish. His own poems have also been translated into Italian, French, German, and Turkish. In October of 2016, Roads Taken, a celebration of the 40th anniversary of Alfred Corn's first book, *All Roads at Once*, was held at Poets House in New York City, and in 2017 he was inducted into the Georgia Writers Hall of Fame. Last year he published a new version Rilke's *Duino Elegies*. He lives in Providence, Rhode Island.

www.ingramcontent.com/pod-product-compliance
Lightning Source LLC
LaVergne TN
LVHW091115080826
845145LV00008B/1924

* 9 7 8 1 9 5 0 4 1 3 4 1 6 *